KT-420-099

BRUSSELS, BRUGES, ANTWERP & GHENT
ENCOUNTER

CATHERINE LE NEVEZ

Brussels, Bruges, Antwerp & Ghent Encounter

Published by Lonely Planet Publications Pty Ltd
ABN 36 005 607 983

Australia	Head Office, Locked Bag 1, Footscray, Vic 3011
	☎ 03 8379 8000 fax 03 8379 8111
	talk2us@lonelyplanet.com.au
USA	150 Linden St, Oakland, CA 94607
	☎ 510 250 6400
	toll free 800 275 8555
	fax 510 893 8572
	info@lonelyplanet.com
UK	2nd fl, 186 City Rd
	London EC1V 2NT
	☎ 020 7106 2100 fax 020 7106 2101
	go@lonelyplanet.co.uk

This title was commissioned in Lonely Planet's London office and produced by: **Commissioning Editor** Caroline Sieg **Coordinating Editor** Laura Crawford **Coordinating Cartographers** Fatima Basic, Tadhgh Knaggs **Assisting Cartographer** Anita Banh **Layout Designer** Cara Smith **Assisting Editor** Trent Holden **Managing Editor** Melanie Dankel **Managing Cartographer** Mark Griffiths **Cover Designer** Amy Stephens **Project Manager** Eoin Dunlevy **Managing Layout Designer** Adam McCrow **Thanks to** Imogen Bannister, Sasha Baskett, Quentin Frayne, Lisa Knights, Chris Love, Adriana Mammarella, Annelies Mertens, Trent Paton, Sally Schafer, Sarah Sloane, Celia Wood

Cover photograph An insider's view – Grand Place, Brussels, Connie Coleman/agephotostock. **Internal photographs** p6, p13, p110 by Annelies Mertens; p25, p51, p175 by Joost de Bock/Getty; p27 by eye35.com/Alamy; p28 by Hemis/Alamy; p20 by Rough Guides/Alamy. All other photographs by Lonely Planet Images, and by Jonathan Smith except p45, p46, p54, p168 by Jean-Bernard Carillet; p4 by Bruce Esbin. All images are copyright of the photographers unless otherwise indicated. Many of the images in this guide are available for licensing from **Lonely Planet Images:** www.lonelyplanetimages.com.

ISBN 978 1 74104 921 3

Printed through Colorcraft Ltd, Hong Kong.
Printed in China.

Acknowledgement Brussels Transit Map ©STIB/MIVB 2008

HOW TO USE THIS BOOK
Colour-Coding & Maps

Colour-coding is used for symbols on maps and in the text that they relate to (eg all eating venues on the maps and in the text are given a green knife and fork symbol). Each neighbourhood and city also gets its own colour, and this is used down the edge of the page and throughout that section.

Shaded yellow areas on the maps denote 'areas of interest' – for their historical significance, their attractive architecture or their great bars and restaurants. We encourage you to head to these areas and just start exploring!

Prices

Multiple prices listed with reviews (eg €10/5 or €10/5/20) indicate adult/child, adult/concession or adult/child/family.

Send us your feedback We love to hear from readers – your comments help make our books better. We read every word you send us, and we always guarantee that your feedback goes straight to the appropriate authors. The most useful submissions are rewarded with a free book. To send us your updates and find out about Lonely Planet events, newsletters and travel news visit our award-winning website: *www.lonelyplanet.com/contact*.

Note: We may edit, reproduce and incorporate your comments in Lonely Planet products such as guidebooks, websites and digital products, so let us know if you don't want your comments reproduced or your name acknowledged. For a copy of our privacy policy visit *www.lonelyplanet.com/privacy*.

CATHERINE LE NEVEZ

Catherine first roadtripped throughout Europe aged four, including her first Belgian foray, and she's been hitting the road here at every opportunity since, completing her Doctorate of Creative Arts in Writing, her Masters in Professional Writing, and post-grad qualifications in editing and publishing along the way.

Catherine's previous writing on Belgium includes Brussels coverage for Lonely Planet's anthology, *The Perfect Day*, and reviews for Lonely Planet's Hotels & Hostels online guide. Elsewhere in Europe, Catherine's authored Lonely Planet's *Paris Encounter* guidebook, and co-authored Lonely Planet's *France, Provence & the Côte d'Azur, Italy, Munich, Bavaria & the Black Forest* and *Ireland* guidebooks.

Belgium – and especially these four cities – remains one of Catherine's favourite places on the planet for its irreverent spirit and its diversity, not to mention its Gandavum Dry Hopping (p152).

CATHERINE'S THANKS

Dank u wel/un grand merci to the wonderful locals and travellers in Brussels, Bruges, Antwerp and Ghent who offered insights and inspiration, including Lucy, 'Dutch Michiel', Koen, Martine, Bridget, Stijn, Bart, Sven and Yam among many (many!) others. At Lonely Planet, cheers to Caroline Sieg for entrusting me with this gig, and to Mark Griffiths and Laura Crawford. As ever, thanks above all to my family.

Our readers Many thanks to the travellers who wrote to us with helpful hints, useful advice and interesting anecdotes. Laurence Anderson, Victoria Bartlett, Juliette Biddall, Ellen Bork, Ian Chapman, Desmond Cumiskey, Annemie Deruytter, Anke Dijkstra, Tineke & Graham Edwards, Jenny Ellis, Stefano Di Felice, Charles V Greenless, Kristin Gustafson, Helen Harjanto, Jarrod Hepburn, Eva Hoffmann, David Howe, Marcel I'Abee, Yuen Ineson, Simon Jackson, Martin Jonsson, Zia Asad Khan, Mark Ladd, Sabine Legrand, Sam Marlows, Kathleen Mccann, Malcolm Mckay, Duane K Meek, Ken & Jan Moore, Robert De Nijs, Martin Nitsch, Michiel Nuyts, Ian Oliver, J Padget, Damien Pentony, Anton Rijsdijk, Jenny Schaffzin, Nancy Scott, Rosemary Sealey, Rebecca Steltner, Jeanine Suurmond, Victoria Svahn, Peter Taylor, Eva Teng, la van Bezecna, Camille van Wessem, Brecht Vergult, Keith Waters, Paul Watson, Barbara Weand, B Weston, Peter Williams, Steve & Judith Willis.

A rooftop view – Bruges cafés

CONTENTS

Our authors are independent, dedicated travellers. They don't research using just the internet or phone, and they don't take freebies, so you can rely on their advice being well researched and impartial. They travel widely visiting thousands of places, taking great pride in getting all the details right and telling it how it is.

THIS IS BRUSSELS, BRUGES, ANTWERP & GHENT

The proximity of Belgium's fab four – the buzzing multinational European capital, Brussels; romantic, canal-woven Bruges; effortlessly cool Antwerp; and laidback, student-filled Ghent – means there's no need to limit your trip to just one of these cities.

Visiting diplomats and coachloads of 'if-it's-Tuesday-this-must-be-Belgium' tourists aren't the only people flitting between these four destinations. Transport between all four cities is frequent and rapid, meaning locals commonly live in Ghent and work in Bruges, for example, or live in Antwerp and commute to Brussels.

Each of the cities has its own unique style, sights and alluring quarters and backstreets. Size also sets them apart: Ghent has roughly double Bruges' population, while in turn Antwerp's population is twice that of Ghent. And Brussels' population, just over twice the size of Antwerp's, doubles again to two million during business hours.

Of course, the four cities have plenty in common too: boats plying the waterways; serene parks; a web of cycling trails; jumbled market stalls; forward-looking fashions; and museums and galleries packed with home-grown art, from the mastery of Rubens to Hergé's Tintin – not to mention beer and chocolate that's lauded as the finest in the world.

This is an especially fascinating time to visit Brussels, Bruges, Antwerp and Ghent, given the peaceful but profound shifting political landscape. At the same time as the country takes an increasingly regional focus, Brussels' outlook is broader than ever before, as the headquarters of an expanding and dynamic EU. Not only are all four of these cities historical treasures whose centuries-old character will endure alongside contemporary innovations, but history is being made here right now.

Top left 99 bottles of beer on the wall…and hundreds more waiting to be emptied (p12) **Top right** Quaint gabled buildings encircle the Markt, Bruges (p99) **Bottom** Brussels' bustling eat street, Rue des Bouchers (p50)

PARAPHARMACIE

Shop in style at the beautiful glass-roofed Galeries St-Hubert, Brussels (p48)

>1 BEER

SIP YOUR WAY THROUGH BELGIUM'S STELLAR RANGE OF BREWS

Sure, Stella Artois and Jupiler need no introduction. But these internationally distributed pilsners are only the beginning, so here's a crash course in Belgian brews.

First things first: beer here is much more than a recipe for a good night out. It is to Belgium what wine is to neighbouring France – something to be savoured slowly, appreciating each brew's individual characteristics and flavours. Appreciating them all could take a while: it's estimated up to 1000 different beers are brewed nationwide. (The exact number's impossible to pin down due to the range of seasonal brews and experimental limited editions.) Each beer has its own unique glass embossed with the beer's logo (marking the level where the head starts) and is specially shaped to enhance the taste and aromas, meaning pouring techniques vary from beer to beer. Even supermarkets sell packaged beer-and-glass sets (most Belgian beers are bottled, rather than on tap).

While monks in France are renowned for winemaking, in Belgium they're devoted to beer. Smooth gold- and dark-coloured Trappist beers – packing 6% to 12% alcohol – have been made for centuries by Trappist (Cistercian) monks. These days, the monks' average age is 70, and there are few new recruits, prompting fears for the beers' future. For now, three abbeys still brew in Flanders (and three in Wallonia); look out for Westmalle Triple, made near Antwerp.

And, in the same way that France has champagne, Belgium has its traditional vintage, the lambic (*lambiek* in Dutch). Like champagne, these sparkling beers take up to three years to make. The secret is wild micro-organisms that inhabit the cold air around the beer, causing spontaneous fermentation. The most popular lambic is the cider-style gueuze (pronounced 'gerze'). They're an acquired taste, but fruit lambics are sweetened with cherry or raspberry, which helps counter the acerbic taste (though steer clear of artificially sweetened quick-brews). In Brussels, try the locally made lambics from Cantillon.

Easier to wash down are pale, cloudy white beers (*witbier* in Dutch, *bière blanche* in French), such as Bruges' Brugs Tarwebier. These are

great iced with lemon in warm weather, unlike many of the country's beers, which are actually best drunk at room temperature.

Belgium also boasts golden ales (led by Duvel); abbey beers (strong, full-flavoured ales, like Leffe, using original abbey recipes though not actually made by monks); Vlaams Rood (Flemish Red beers, aged in wooden barrels); and sour-tasting Oud Bruin (Old Brown beers, blending young and old beers, with a secondary fermentation in the bottle).

The world is finally tapping into Belgium's bountiful beers – exports to the US alone in 2007 were up 83% on the previous year (but cost on average 60% more there than in Belgium).

For a rundown of the best places to taste-test Belgium's beers in the four cities and the local beer-drinking etiquette, see p164.

>2 CHOCOLATE

CHOOSE THE PERFECT BOX OF BELGIAN CHOCOLATES

Wafting aromas of warm, sweet, melting chocolate seduce you first. Then you catch sight of the rows of glinting light brown, dark brown and creamy-white coated squares, oblongs, balls and cups; some embossed with a gold stamp, others with elaborate swirls, and still more wrapped in shimmering tinfoil or twisted inside cellophane. A white-gloved assistant runs through each one's composition – from *crème fraîche* (fresh whipped-cream filling) to *ganache* (blended chocolate, fresh cream and extra cocoa butter flavoured with coffee, cinnamon or liqueurs) – then painstakingly hand-picks them one at a time and pops them into a *ballotin* (a special, stylised box).

Yes, even shopping for chocolate is an art here in Belgium – which it would want to be, with premium chocolates pushing €120 per kilo.

All up, Belgium produces a whopping 220,000 tonnes of chocolate per year. Its unmatched reputation for sublime chocolate derives from the silky-smooth texture created by extended conching (stirring), and from the use of pure cocoa butter. The history of how Belgium came to acquire this fundamental ingredient is far from sweet, however, as it's directly linked to King Léopold II's invasion of the Congo, which facilitated easy access to Africa's cocoa fields. Like many Belgian chocolates, Côte d'Or was first made in 1885 when

elephants transported cocoa beans through the tropical jungle, hence the elephant on its packaging. These days, chocolate makers increasingly work within Fairtrade practices.

A turning point for Belgian chocolate came in 1912, when pralines (filled chocolates) were born in Brussels. Today these are undergoing another evolution at the hands of the country's mould-breaking chocolatiers. Fusion pralines incorporate fantastical flavours such as Havana cigar, cauliflower, green pea, chilli and wasabi. This is where being able to select chocolates individually comes in handy: you can experiment without consigning yourself to a boxful.

In addition to the rarefied showrooms of top chocolatiers like Brussels' Pierre Marcolini (p61), Bruges' Dominique Persoone (p107), and Antwerp's Burie (p127) and Del Rey (p128), there are also numerous luxury chains. Côte d'Or, the now US-owned Godiva and the rippled, mottled seashells produced by Guylian are the best known internationally. Popular local manufacturers include Leonidas, the original praline creator Neuhaus (p48) and Corné, as well as Galler, which also offers its superb pralines (such as fresh pistachio-filled white chocolate) in chocolate-bar form. You'll also find many of these top chain brands in supermarkets for a fraction of the price you pay at the boutiques.

Temptation prevails right until leaving the country – Brussels International Airport is the biggest chocolate-selling point in the world.

See p174 for the cities' best chocolate shops.

>3 COMICS

REACQUAINT YOURSELF WITH LOCAL ICONS LIKE TINTIN AND THE SMURFS

Getting comical in Belgium is serious business. Belgians called comics the 'ninth art' (after architecture, sculpture, painting, music, dance, poetry, film and TV), and even in today's multimedia-saturated environment, comics (or 'graphic novels' as they're often called outside Belgium) continue to churn off the press. Often today's adult-aimed comics have a political bent, such as *Brüsel* from François Schuiten and Benoit Peeters' *Les Cités Obscures* series, about an old city destroyed by the new – a metaphor for the EU's impact on the capital.

Comics kicked off in Belgium around the same time as the Art Nouveau movement, and the two genres are intertwined at the country's national museum for comics, Brussels' Centre Belge de la Bande Dessinée (Belgian Comic Strip Centre; p41), housed in a light-filled former textile warehouse designed by Victor Horta. The centre illustrates the production of comics, and, among others, has permanent exhibits dedicated to the Smurfs (*Les Schtroumpf;* yes, they're Belgian, not French, created by Brussels-born Pierre Culliford, aka Peyo in 1948), and the most famous Belgian comic character of all, Tintin. The artist behind this hugely popular series, Georges Remi, known as Hergé (whose nom de plume comes from the reversal of his initials), was also born in Brussels, and his cub reporter's adventures depict world journeys and events, launching with *Tintin in the Land of the Soviets*

LARGER-THAN-LIFE COMICS

Walking through Brussels' streets is like stepping into the pages of a larger-than-life comic book. Throughout the city, Brussels' Comic Strip Route connects an ever-expanding series of giant comic murals, with around 50 to date. The 6km trail is detailed in a free brochure from Brussels' tourist office (downloadable from www.brusselsinternational.be) and takes about three hours. In any event, keep an eye out for these colourful murals popping into view as you round the city's corners, and go into its nooks and crannies. Comic murals recently started springing up in Antwerp's city centre too, initiated by comic shop/gallery **Mekanik Strip** (p130).

(1929–30), followed by *Tintin in the Congo* (1930–31), which remains a contentious depiction of Belgium's occupation of its former colony. The album was redrawn in 1946, during which time Hergé removed several colonial references, but controversy lingers today about its political correctness. Hergé's later works would go on to incorporate meticulous cultural and historical research.

Other Belgian comic-strip icons include Suske and Wiske (Bob and Bobette) created by Antwerp artist Willy Vandersteen in 1945; Lucky Luke, by Maurice De Bevère, aka Morris, in 1946; and Nero by Marc Sleen in 1947.

Many of these comic characters, among countless others, are immortalised as part of Brussels' Comic Strip Route (see opposite). Throughout Brussels, Bruges, Antwerp and Ghent, you'll come across dozens of shops specialising in comics; see the Shop sections of each city.

>4 FASHION

OVERHAUL YOUR WARDROBE WITH CUTTING-EDGE BELGIAN DESIGNS

With its artistic legacy and history of cloth trading, Belgium was destined to storm European catwalks.

The country's relatively recent rise is credited to the Antwerp Six – Ann Demeulemeester (p127), Dries Van Noten (see Het Modepaleis, p130), Walter Van Beirendonck (p131), Dirk Van Saene, Dirk Bikkembergs and Marina Yee – who studied together at Antwerp's Royal Academy of Fine Arts. In 1987 they trucked their wildly diverse designs across the channel to stage an audacious show in London. Its stratospheric success was due to a combination of uninhibited talent and savvy marketing – individually their names didn't lend themselves to easy recognition, but the catch-all labelling captured the media's imagination and put Antwerp on the international map. The academy's resulting prestige attracted new generations of talent, boutiques set up shop, waves of fashion buyers and shoppers flooded in, and, eventually, even famously modest Belgians realised they were stealing Paris' and Milan's thunder.

Though worth millions, Belgium's fashion industry is still resolutely independent. Antwerp remains at its epicentre, with a striking fashion museum, MoMu (p123) sharing space with the academy in the Mode-Natie in the city's fashion quarter (p128). Beyond Antwerp, the scene also continues to flourish, with home-grown designers' boutiques in Bruges, Ghent, and especially along Brussels' Rue Antoine Dansaert. See the Shop sections in each city for shopping hotspots, and the interview with Bart Willems (p129) for a peek behind the scenes.

>5 BOAT CRUISES

CRUISE THE WATERWAYS FOR A PEACEFUL PERSPECTIVE OF THE CITIES

Of these four cities, Bruges is best known for its picturesque canals meandering between Gothic buildings. But it's not the only place where you can get out on the water. Ghent's confluence of rivers and canals lace together its graceful old town. And although many of Brussels' original canals are now underground, you can board a boat for a view of the capital's industrialised waterways. Antwerp may not have canals, but it does have the mighty Scheldt river, which has given rise to its booming port (Europe's second largest, and the fourth largest in the world).

Cruise details are listed on p195. Bear in mind that the fickle weather means that even in summer it can get chilly out on deck – bring a jacket whatever the season.

>6 JENEVER

SAMPLE BELGIUM'S SPIRITED PRECURSOR TO GIN

Belgium may be internationally synonymous with beer, but locally it's also equally known for its *jenever* (*genièvre* in French). This potent combination of grain spirit, juniper berries and grasses has been distilled in Belgium since medieval times, when it was used as a medicine. Once it made its way to Britain, its name and taste evolved into gin.

Like beer, it's impossible to pin down just how many *jenevers* are made in Belgium but it's estimated at somewhere approaching 300, spanning an astonishing range of flavours. It's a matter of personal taste, of course, but sweet fruit flavours such as raspberry can tend to taste like cough mixture, whereas less sugary varieties like sour apple or cactus (yes, cactus) are more thirst quenching. Being Belgian, this original gin also comes in chocolate flavours.

Like beer, too, *jenever* is intended to be sipped slowly, despite being served in shot glasses. In any case, it's strong stuff, averaging around 35% alcohol; the most potent, Thor apple, is a whopping 53%.

Jenevers are characterised as either *jonge* (young) or *oude* (old), although confusingly, this doesn't refer to their age, but rather the ingredients and distilling techniques. That said, aged *jenevers* of either kind are best.

See also p164 for the best spots to taste them yourself.

>7 CYCLING

JOIN THE LOCALS BY GETTING ON YER BIKE

'Bikes are holy here,' locals will warn you, and it's true. This is bad news if you're a driver or even a pedestrian (be prepared to leap out of the way!), but great news if you're cycling yourself.

The area of Flanders encompassing Brussels, Bruges, Antwerp and Ghent is primarily flat, making cycling a calf-friendly way to get around. Added to that, bike lanes run through the cities, there's no shortage of places to park your bike safely, and bike hire is cheap and getting cheaper, including a new initiative by the City of Brussels that allows you to pick up and drop off bikes at 'bike stations' around town at an incredibly low hourly rate – see p191. Brussels even celebrates cycling culture with an annual festival, Dring Dring – see p28. You can also sightsee at the same time on organised cycling tours (p195).

If city cycling doesn't inspire you, try the cycling paths that also weave through the cities' parks, or you can head further afield, such as to the Belgian coast (p108), less than an hour's pedalling from Bruges.

Bike rental outlets in the four cities are listed on p191.

HIGHLIGHTS

>8 MARKETS

HUNT FOR TREASURES AT THE COLOURFUL MARKETS

Arming yourself with an empty suitcase is a smart move, not only for designer fashions, chocolate and specialist beers, but for the unexpected finds at the cities' array of markets.

The full spectrum of markets set up regularly in Brussels, Bruges, Antwerp and Ghent – from elegant antiques markets and fairs trading rare china, crystal and furniture, through to flea markets spilling over with *brocante* (bric-a-brac) and secondhand treasures, such as dog-eared comics, CDs and old vinyl records, plus new and vintage clothing. There are also rainbow-like food markets where you can pick up picnic ingredients.

Christmas season brings the most magical markets of all, when the cities' ancient squares fill with stalls selling handcrafted toys, nutcrackers, a dazzling array of ornaments and warming mugs of sweet mulled wine. Winter wonderlands of ice sculptures and outdoor skating rinks are erected most years (both generally take place throughout the month of December). Tourist offices can advise the markets' venues, but you can't go wrong by just following the crowds.

Any time of year, the street fare sold from caravans parked at the markets is a treat: steaming waffles that tickle your nose (p51) and cones full of mayonnaise-slathered fries (p69).

See the Shop sections of each city chapter for a rundown of the cities' markets.

>9 JAZZ

SWING TO A LIVE JAZZ SESSION

What do Adolphe Sax, Jean 'Toots' Thielemans, Django Reinhardt and Jacques Brel have in common? They've all played an instrumental role in the evolution of jazz…and they're all Belgian. Sax invented the saxophone here in 1846. Legendary harmonica player Thielemans shared the stage with Ella Fitzgerald, Quincy Jones and Paul Simon, among others (and even now that he's aged in his 80s, he still continues to enthral audiences). Reinhardt's electrifying performances in the early 20th century immortalised him as one of the greatest jazz guitarists of all time. And crooner Brel catapulted to fame in 1950s France but retained a strong affinity for his homeland, as documented at Fondation Jaques Brel p41.

Their legacy has led to a thriving scene today, with jazz clubs and performances proliferating throughout Brussels, Bruges, Antwerp and Ghent – see p172 for stand-out venues.

Numerous jazz festivals take place in the cities, including the Brussels Jazz Marathon (p27) each May, when hundreds of artists perform all over the capital, and during Antwerp's biennial Jazz Middelheim (p26), featuring high-standard performers.

>10 DIAMONDS

GET THE NITTY-GRITTY ON DIAMOND CUTTING, POLISHING AND TRADING

Exiting Antwerp's resplendently restored train station you may need your sunglasses for the diamond shops lining its halls. But heading a little deeper into its diamond quarter, especially along the pedestrianised streets of Shupstraat, Hoveniersstraat and Rijfstraat, brings you to a less glitzy world where diamonds are traded on the street, institutes are concealed behind steely grills, and unassuming *beurzen voor diamanthandel* (diamond exchanges) contain millions of dollars worth of stones.

Over 70% of the world's rough diamonds are traded in these high-security Antwerp backstreets, home to four diamond exchanges and 1500 diamond companies. Traditionally the domain of Orthodox Jews, these days up to 60% of those working in the industry are Indian; which accounts for the Bank of India's presence here. Deals aren't done on paper, but are sealed by a handshake and the traditional Jewish term *mazal,* meaning 'good luck'.

On average, diamonds cost 20% less at retail boutiques in Antwerp, where they can be sourced instantly, than elsewhere in Belgium and beyond. Nonshoppers can still learn about them at Antwerp's lustrous Diamantmuseum (Diamond Museum; p119), and watch diamond cutters at work at Diamondland (p123). You can also see these jewels being polished in the medieval cellar of the Diamantmuseum (p104) in Bruges, where diamond-polishing techniques were invented in the 15th century before the industry shifted to Antwerp.

>DIARY

Not even the notoriously fickle climate can rain on Belgium's parade when it's time to party. Brussels, Bruges, Antwerp and Ghent each host a slew of diverse events, especially midyear. And the short distances between the cities means you're only a train ride away from some sort of festivity.

In addition to the tourist offices' websites (p197), good places to find out what's on where include the *What's On* supplement in the weekly English-language magazine the *Bulletin* (www .thebulletin.be), and *Agenda* (www.brusselsagenda.be), a lively events magazine published weekly in English, French and Dutch. Many festival dates vary from year to year; check the websites for details.

People get into the spirit after dark in Brussels

JANUARY

New Year's celebrations, Brussels

January begins with a bang when midnight fireworks explode from Mont des Arts. Revellers also ring in the New Year on Brussels' Grand Place.

FEBRUARY

Anima, Brussels & Ghent

http://folioscope.awn.com

Brussels' animated film festival attracts top-quality shorts and features, and mounts exhibitions, workshops and lectures – then hits the road for other cities including Ghent.

MARCH

Cinema Novo Film Festival, Bruges

www.cinemanovo.be

Independent films from Asia, Africa and Latin America take to the screen in early to mid-March with the aim of presenting developing nations' cultures in an insightful new light.

Ars Musica, Brussels

www.arsmusica.be

Audiences get wired into the contemporary music scene at this accessible festival through rehearsals with public feedback, roundtable discussions, documentary film projections and concert introductions.

APRIL

Choco-Laté, Bruges

www.choco-late.be

Some years see a small chocolate market, others a full-blown festival with everything from tastings to chocolate beauty-treatments, chocolate-and-wine pairing and a 'kids village'.

BEST BIENNIALS

The country's biggest cultural extravaganza, Brussels' **Europalia** (www.europalia.be), encompasses visual arts, music, theatre and dance, and lasts for four months (generally October of odd-numbered years through to February of even-numbered years).

In late May of even-numbered years don't miss Brussels' zany one-day parade, **Zinneke** (www.zinneke.org, in Dutch & French), a kind of urban, ultra-contemporary 'street opera' featuring outlandish handmade costumes.

A magical rotating carpet of 800,000 begonias blankets Brussels' Grand Place during the **Tapis des Fleurs** (www.flowercarpet.be) for four days in August of even-numbered years.

August of odd-numbered years heralds Antwerp's week-long **Jazz Middelheim** (www.jazzmiddelheim.be), one of the city's biggest shindigs.

Wall-to-wall begonia carpet colours Brussels' Grand Place during the Tapis des Fleurs (opposite)

MAY

Les Nuits Botanique, Brussels
www.lesnuits.be, in French & Dutch
Twelve days of rock, reggae, ska, hip-hop, electro, folk, rap, blues and more in Brussels' Jardin Botanique.

Belgian Lesbian & Gay Pride, Brussels
www.blgp.be
'Rainbow Week' in mid-May centres on 'Pink Saturday', an over-the-top glamour parade followed by all-night clubbing.

Brussels Jazz Marathon, Brussels
www.brusselsjazzmarathon.be
Get bussed free to 125 gratis city-wide concerts, featuring 400-plus artists over three jazz-fuelled days in late May.

Kunsten Festival des Arts, Brussels
www.kunstenfestivaldesarts.be
Kunsten's visual and performing arts events strive to redefine Belgium's national, linguistic and cultural borders.

Ommegang brings out the medieval in these Bruxellois

Dring Dring Bike Festival, Brussels

www.dringdring.be, in Dutch & French
Buy new and secondhand bikes, learn to navigate city traffic, and take guided trips or – if you missed out as a kid – adult cycling lessons.

JUNE

Beerpassie Weekend, Antwerp

www.beerpassion.com, in Dutch
Sample upwards of 150 stellar beers including brand-new creations at Antwerp's mid-June three-day celebration of brewing.

Couleur Café Festival, Brussels

www.couleurcafe.be
Performers at this three-day world music and dance knees-up in late June have included James Brown and UB40.

JULY

Ommegang, Brussels

www.ommegang.be

Dating from the 14th century, this medieval-style procession kicks off from the Place du Grand Sablon, ending with a dance in the illuminated Grand Place.

Belgium National Day celebrations, Brussels

www.belgium.be

Concerts and events centred on the capital's Parc de Bruxelles commemorate Leopold I becoming Belgium's first king on 21 July 1831.

Gentse Feesten, Ghent

www.gentsefeesten.be

Europe's largest street festival turns Ghent into a dedicated hedonists' zone, with music, outdoor theatre and plenty of beer flowing. Gentse Feesten incorporates several parallel festivals, including *10 Days Off* (www.10daysoff.be) in late July – a frenzy of house, electro, breakbeats, rock, drum 'n' bass, techno, funk, disco and much more.

Sfinks Festival, Antwerp

www.sfinks.be

True-to-its-roots four-day world music festival with a chilled atmosphere and an impressively diverse range of artists.

AUGUST

Klinkers, Bruges

www.klinkers-brugge.be

Eleven-day music fest culminating in *Benewerk* (legwork), featuring dancing from salsa to folk to '80s.

Brussels Marathon, Brussels

www.sport.be/brusselsmarathon

Join the thousands pounding the capital's cobblestones, or just cheer them on from the sidelines.

Musica Antiqua, Bruges

www.festival.be

This festival of early music not only includes concerts but hands-on workshops like harpsichord maintenance.

Brussels Summer Festival, Brussels

www.infofestival.be

Free 10-day bash packing in more than 140 different performances (concerts, children's theatre and more), including lots of local acts.

SEPTEMBER

Belgian Beer Weekend, Brussels

www.weekenddelabiere.be

The Grand Place is overtaken by a veritable village of stalls selling beer and associated paraphernalia (glasses, coasters etc). Drink prices are reasonable and entry is free.

Nuit Blanche, Brussels

www.brusselsinternational.be

For one 'white night', the capital stays up until sunrise, laying on a swathe of events including projections, installations, circus acts and parties.

OCTOBER

Comics Festival, Brussels

www.comicsfestivalbelgium.com

Rub shoulders with the artists and writers behind some of Belgium's best-known comic characters.

NOVEMBER

International Independent Film Festival, Brussels

www.centremultimedia.org

In answer to commercialised schlock, independent filmmakers from 60 countries screen over 100 innovative films over one week in early November.

DECEMBER

Christmas markets, all cities

www.visitbelgium.be

Warm up throughout December with a steaming mug of mulled wine while browsing fairy-tale stalls stocked with handcrafted toys and ornaments. See also p22.

Bruges' serene Minnewater park (p101)

ITINERARIES

You can, of course, concentrate on just exploring one of these intriguing cities. But because they're so close to each other, it's easy to mix-and-match several during the same trip. If you're planning a long weekend, start on a Friday, as most Belgian museums (and some shops) shut on Monday.

BRUSSELS IN ONE DAY

The gilded façades encircling Brussels' splendid Grand Place (p44) glint in the early morning sun, making it a picturesque spot to kick off a tour of the capital. While here, pop into the city's history museum, Musée de la Ville de Bruxelles (p46), then stroll through the glass-roofed Galeries St-Hubert (p48) to Brussels' cathedral (p57) and its finest museums – check out the Musée BELvue (p57) and the Musées Royaux des Beaux-Arts (p60). While in this area, time your trip to the Musée des Instruments de Musique (p57) for lunch at its rooftop café. Take the glass lift outside the colossal Palais de Justice (p60) to the Marolles (p82) to dine at one of its renowned restaurants – try Comme Chez Soi (p86) – before hitting its clubs (p87).

BRUSSELS IN TWO DAYS

Browse the Belgian designer boutiques (p90) along Rue Antoine Dansaert and watch chess players battling it out at Le Greenwich (p97). Lunch at one of St-Catherine's seafood restaurants (p92) before appraising architecture at the space-age Atomium (p91), the EU quarter (p64), or Victor Horta's Art Nouveau home-turned-museum, the Musée Horta (p77). Refuel at one of the buzzing restaurants (p80) on Rue St-Boniface, then head to Place Flagey (p81) for a cocktail at Café Belga (p80), then a film at Studio 5 (p81), a concert (p81) or catch a session at Sounds Jazz Club (p81).

Top left Not-so-hidden treasures await at the Place du Jeu-de-Balle market, Brussels (p86) **Top right** Life's cruisy on the Rozenhoedkaai, Bruges (p99) **Bottom** Colour your world at the Centre Belge de la Bande Dessinée, Brussels (p41)

ITINERARIES

BRUGES IN ONE DAY

Stroll past the colonnaded fish market (p111) and along the canals or cruise them instead (p195). Get a bird's-eye view of the city from the top of the Belfort (p101) then descend to the ruins of St-Donaas (p104). Watch diamonds being polished at the Diamantmuseum (p104) before joining the locals lunching at Nieuw Museum (p112). Admire art from the Flemish Primitives to the surrealists at the Groeningemuseum (p104) and take time out in the serene Begijnhof (p101) before touring the working de Halve Maan brewery (p101). Enjoy a meal at Den Dyver (p112), where beer is not only paired with each dish, but is also a key cooking ingredient. For yet more Belgian brews, head back below ground to 't Poatersgat (p114).

ANTWERP IN ONE DAY

Stroll through Antwerp's diamond district (p24) and along the shop-lined Meir (p127) to Antwerp's cathedral (p125) to view Rubens' canvases before visiting his home, the Rubenshuis (p126). Fashion fiends should hit the Mode Museum (p123), while Art Nouveau fans might zip out for a stroll around Zurenborg (p122), or dine amid the wrought-iron girders

Rubens shows the way to the Gothic Onze Lieve Vrouwekathedraal, Antwerp (p125)

FORWARD PLANNING

Three weeks before you go Hook up with locals via websites such as Tof People and Like a Local (see Insider Information p62), and check out events calendars (p25) to see what's on where and try to secure tickets.

One to two weeks before you go Book a table at one of the cities' gastronomic restaurants (see the Eat sections of each city), buy a Brussels Card online for city-wide savings including on public transport (p192), and whet your palate with some pre-trip research on Belgian beers (p194).

One day before you go Pack your comfiest shoes for tramping the cities' cobblestones (you'll be glad you did!).

at Grand Café Horta (p132). After absorbing the city's maritime history (p125), take the St-Anna pedestrian tunnel (p127) to the river's western bank for superb skyline views. After checking out 't Zuid's Fotomuseum (p123) and Koninklijk Museum voor Schone Kunsten (p123), stick around for its restaurants, bars and clubs – or a combination of all three, such as Stereo Sushi (p140).

GHENT IN ONE DAY

Board a boat (p196) to see Ghent's gracious cityscapes from the rivers and canals bisecting the city, then head to the Belfort (p144) to see them from above. After touring Ghent's ancient castle, Gravensteen (p144), marvel over Jan Van Eyck's masterpiece, *The Adoration of the Mystic Lamb* (p145), then check out art of a completely different kind on 'Graffiti Street' (p147). More art awaits at the Museum voor Schone Kunsten (p144) and the radical contemporary gallery, SMAK (p146). Settle on a restaurant in the tangled laneways of Patershol (p150). Be sure not to miss two unique Ghent drinking experiences – 't Velootje (p153) for its atmosphere, and Het Waterhuis aan de Bierkant (p152) for its house brews. And don't miss a stroll through the floodlit city by night (p154).

Be floored by Brussels' stunning Grand Place

BRUSSELS NEIGHBOURHOODS

Visitors expecting to fall for Brussels at first sight are often disenchanted. The secret to Brussels is that its attractions are scattered throughout the city's diverse quarters, and seeking them out rewards you with an appreciation of Europe's multi-faceted capital that's much more than skin deep.

Brussels' innate contradictions confound expectations. This is one of the world's truly international yet least-globalised cities. You won't find a single Starbucks or Burger King, but neither is it all Belgian waffles and *frites*. The city's multinational make-up stems from the fact that a quarter of its one million residents are foreigners (in addition to diplomatic, business and leisure travellers), which accounts for its incredible variety of shops, cuisines and entertainment, and the multitude of languages spoken on its streets. English is increasingly the neutral lingua franca of young Dutch-speaking and Francophone Bruxellois, and is even mooted by some to become the capital's third official language in the future.

This cosmopolitan character is reinforced by Brussels' compact size. Bounded by an outer ring road, an inner ring road defines the historic centre, which splits topographically into the Lower Town (the medieval core) and the Upper Town (to the Grand Place's east and southeast).

In this book, we've divided the city into six neighbourhoods. The cobbled Grand Place and Îlot Sacré quarter is Brussels' geographic heart. To its southeast, the Royal quarter and Sablon are awash with monumental buildings and chocolate and antique shops. Further east is the gleaming EU quarter and Etterbeek, and museum-filled Parc du Cinquantenaire. Heading southwest you'll find the Art Nouveau–adorned Matongé, Ixelles and St-Gilles quarter, encompassing Brussels' African and student communities, ultra-luxe shops and hip bars. North of here is the old working-class Marolles neighbourhood, which is rapidly gentrifying. North again is the Ste-Catherine and St-Géry quarter, where fashion ateliers and trendy cafés neighbour traditional seafood merchants and timeworn watering holes. Further afield lie several intriguing areas worth the trip.

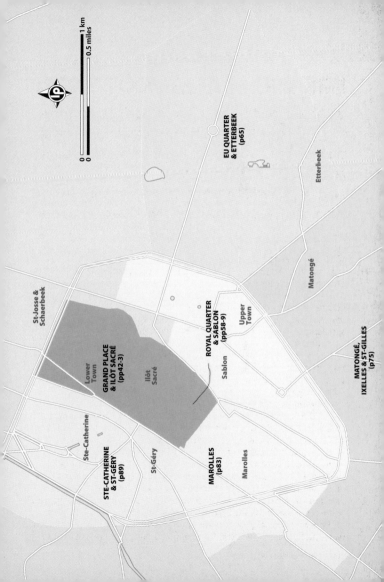

0 1 km
0 0.5 miles

St-Josse &
Schaerbeek

Lower
Town

GRAND PLACE
& ILÔT SACRÉ
(pp42-3)

Îlot
Sacré

Ste-Catherine

STE-CATHERINE
& ST-GÉRY (p89)

St-Géry

MAROLLES
(p83)

Marolles

Sablon

ROYAL QUARTER
& SABLON
(pp58-9)

Upper
Town

MATONGÉ,
IXELLES & ST-GILLES
(p75)

Matongé

EU QUARTER
& ETTERBEEK
(p65)

Etterbeek

>GRAND PLACE & ILÔT SACRÉ

Brussels' heart beats on its main square, the Grand Place. Ringed by gold-trimmed, gabled houses built by merchant guilds, and flanked by the city's 15th-century Gothic town hall (Hôtel de Ville), this iconic square is considered to be Europe's most magnificent.

The Grand Place's cobblestones were first laid in the 12th century, when it was used as a Grote Markt (marketplace); the names of the narrow lanes in this area still evoke herbs, cheese, poultry and the like. During the 1960s' building boom, these medieval lanes were threatened with demolition, prompting proprietors to establish the 'free commune' of Ilôt Sacré to preserve the lanes' architectural character. Today many lanes are undeniably touristy, but have a lively atmosphere nonetheless.

Surrounding this historic core you'll find traditional wood-panelled cafés, beautiful glass-covered shopping arcades and many of the city's key sights including another Brussels icon, Manneken Pis.

GRAND PLACE & ILÔT SACRÉ

◎ SEE
Centre Belge de la Bande
  Dessinée.........................1 E3
Fondation Jacques Brel..2 C7
Hôtel de Ville...................3 B6
Jeanneke Pis....................4 C5
Manneken Pis...................5 B6
Musée de la Brasserie.....6 C6
Musée de la Ville de
  Bruxelles.......................7 C5
Musée du Cacao et du
  Chocolat........................8 B5
Musée du Costume et
  de la Dentelle................9 C6
Scientastic Museum.....10 B5

⬛ SHOP
Boutique Tintin............11 C6
City 2............................12 D2
De Biertempel...............13 C5
Delvaux........................14 C5

FNAC.....................(see 12)
Galeries St-Hubert......15 D5
Neuhaus.......................16 C5
Passage du Nord..........17 C3
Planète Chocolat.........18 B6
Sterling Books..............19 C4
Waterstones................20 D2

⬛ EAT
Arcadi...........................21 D5
Brasserie de la Roue
  d'Or.............................22 C6
Dandoy.........................23 B6
Kokob..........................24 A6
La Maison du Cygne 25 C6
Pita Outlets.................26 C6
Sea Grill.......................27 D4

⬛ DRINK
À la Bécasse.................28 B5
À la Mort Subite 29 D5

Au Soleil 30 A6
Falstaff.........................31 B5
Fontainas.....................32 A6
Goupil le Fol 33 C6
Le Cirio........................34 B5

⭐ PLAY
Actor's Studio...............35 C5
Ancienne Belgique.......36 B5
Arenberg Galeries 37 C5
Duke's..........................38 C6
Le You..........................39 C6
The Music Village.........40 B5
Théâtre du Vaudeville..41 C5
Théâtre National...........42 C2
Théâtre Royal de la
  Monnaie/Koninklijke
  Muntschouwburg........43 C4
Théâtre Royal de
  Toone...........................44 C5

Please see over for map

SEE

CENTRE BELGE DE LA BANDE DESSINÉE

☎ 02 219 19 80; www.comicscenter
.net, in Dutch & French; Rue des Sables
20; adult/concession €7.50/6; ⏰ 10am-
6pm Tue-Sun; Ⓜ Rogier; ♿

Belgium's national Comic Strip
Centre is a studious look at the
evolution of comics: how they're
made, seminal artists and their
creations, and contemporary
comic-strip artists. In truth, the
admission price is steep for the
rather limited displays – unless
you're an Art Nouveau aficion-
ado, in which case it's worth
visiting to see Victor Horta's 1906
light-filled glass-and-steel textile
warehouse in which the museum
is housed. Few interpretive signs
are in English; ask to borrow an
English-language booklet. There is
also a comprehensive shop selling
comics, and a pleasant café.

FONDATION JACQUES BREL

☎ 02 511 10 20; www.jacquesbrel.be;
Place de la Vieille Halle aux Blés 11;
adult/concession/under 12 yr €5/3.50/
free; ⏰ 10.30am-6pm Tue-Sat; Ⓜ Gare
Centrale

Chansonnier Jacques Brel
(1929–78) made his debut in 1952
at a cabaret in his native Belgium,
and shot to fame in Paris, where
he was a contemporary of Édith

Things get graphic at the Comic Strip Centre

Piaf and co, though his songs con-
tinued to hark back to the bleak
'flat land' of his native country.
This dedicated archive centre and
museum, set up by his daughter,
France (named for Brel's adopted
home), contains more than a hundred hours of footage and another
hundred of audio recordings, as
well as thousands of photographs
and articles.

HÔTEL DE VILLE

Grand Place; tours €3; ⏰ 45 min tours
in English 3.15pm Tue & Wed year-round,
12.15pm Sun Apr-Sep; Ⓜ Gare Centrale
or premetro Bourse

Ironically, Brussels' gargoyled,
Gothic-style town hall,

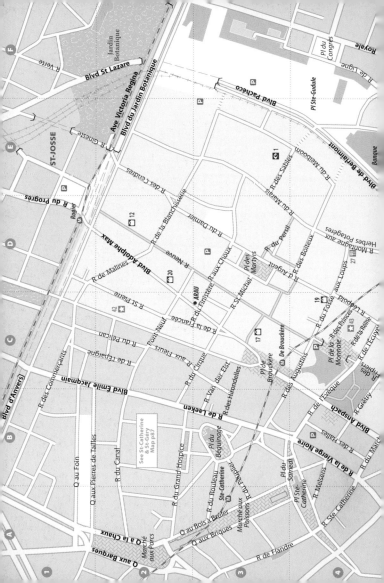

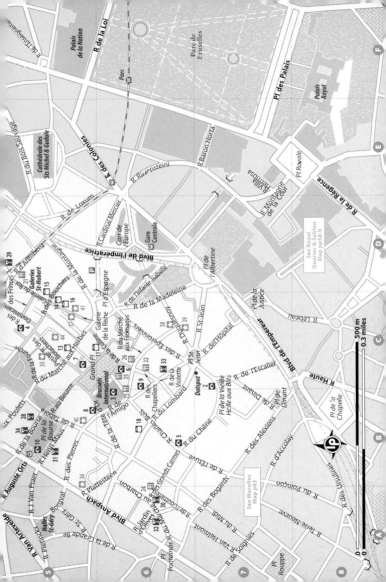

GRAND PLACE GUILDHALLS

The original half-timbered merchant guilds' buildings now surrounding Grand Place were wiped out during the 1695 French bombardment, but rebuilt from stone within five years. Look closely for decorative detail on the façades attesting to the following guilds:

> No 1: Maison des Boulangers (Bakers' House) Bakers
> No 2: La Brouette (The Wheelbarrow) Grease-makers
> No 4: Le Sac (The Bag) Cabinet-makers
> No 5: La Louve (The She-Wolf) Archers
> No 6: Le Cornet (The Horn) Boatmen
> No 7: Le Renard (The Fox) Haberdashers
> No 9: Le Cygne (The Swan) Butchers
> No 10: L'Arbre d'Or (The Golden Tree) Brewers
> Nos 26 & 27: Le Pigeon (The Pigeon) Artists

constructed in 1402, was the only building on the Grand Place to escape the 1695 French bombardment, despite being the intended target. Adorned with stone reliefs of nobility, its 96m-high tower is topped by a gilded statue of St Michel, the city's patron saint. Today it houses the city's tourist office, Brussels International (see p197).

◎ JEANNEKE PIS
Impasse de la Fidélité; Ⓜ Gare Centrale or premetro Bourse
Squatting just off Rue des Bouchers, this pigtailed female counterpart of Manneken Pis (right) is the work of sculptor Denis Adrien Debouvrie, who installed her here in 1985, though she's usually partly obscured by locked iron gates.

◎ MANNEKEN PIS
Cnr Rue de l'Étuve & Rue du Chêne; Ⓜ Gare Centrale or premetro Bourse; ♿
Situated three souvenir-shop-lined blocks from the Grand Place is the little lad himself, sculpted by Jerôme Duquesnoy. The tourist office (in Hôtel de Ville, p41) can tell you when he'll be dressed in one of his costumes (on display at the Musée de la Ville de Bruxelles, p46), at which time this youthful fountain sometimes spouts beer or wine instead of water. See also opposite.

◎ MUSÉE DE LA BRASSERIE
☎ 02 511 49 87; www.beerparadise.be; Grand Place 10; admission €5; ⏲ 10am-5pm daily Apr-Nov, noon-5pm Sat & Sun Dec-Mar; Ⓜ Gare Centrale or premetro Bourse

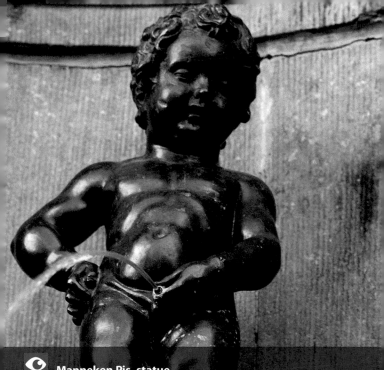

Manneken Pis, statue

Real name? Petit Julien (Little Julian). **Why are you here?** Some say I was extinguishing a fire; others say I was lost and my dad, a nobleman, found me like this and was so relieved himself he had me installed here. I don't remember – I've been here since 1619, after all. Before becoming bronze I was here in stone from the mid-14th century. But I still feel like a five year old. **You're very small and, people often feel, very underwhelming, given your fame.** I'm 30cm! Besides, I'm ironic…it's the local sense of humour. Anyway, look at the thousands of tourists photographing me. **Done much travelling?** Yep, I've been stolen several times. **Relatives living in Brussels?** My sister, Jeanneke Pis (opposite), and dog, Zinneke (p90); incontinence runs in the family. **Will Belgium ever split?** I suppose I could be cloned again, if need be. Regardless, I'll stay put.

BRUSSELS

GRAND PLACE & ILÔT SACRÉ

Brussels' brewery museum is authentic in the sense that it occupies the basement of the brewers' guildhall and has some 18th-century brewing equipment. But visitors are often disappointed at its small size and the lack of any actual brewing taking place (though you do get a beer at the end). To see a real brewery in action, head to the Cantillon Brewery's Musée Bruxellois de la Gueuze (p84).

☉ MUSÉE DE LA VILLE DE BRUXELLES

☎ 02 279 43 50; www.brucity.be; Maison du Roi, Grand Place; adult/concession €3/2.50; ☺ 10am-5pm Tue-Sun; Ⓜ Gare Centrale or premetro Bourse

No king actually ever lived in this Maison du Roi (King's House), but in the folklore section of Brussels' City Museum are 760-odd regal costumes – including an Elvis suit – belonging to Manneken Pis (p44), whose official dresser cloaks him in these little outfits on special occasions. Other museum highlights include Pieter Breugel the Elder's *Cortège de Noces* (Wedding Procession; 1567), along with maps and paintings tracing the history of the city.

More Tintin than you can poke a waffle at

MUSÉE DU CACAO ET DU CHOCOLAT

☎ 02 514 20 48; www.mucc.be; Rue de la Tête d'Or 9; adult/concession/under 12 yr €5/4/free; ⏰ 10am-4.30pm daily Jul & Aug, 10am-4.30pm Tue-Sun Sep-Jun; Ⓜ Gare Centrale or premetro Bourse

Exhibits at Brussels' museum of cocoa and chocolate give you a quick rundown of chocolate's history in Europe, along with chocolate's anti-aging and antidepressant properties. A couple of small treats along the way include a tasting at the praline-making demonstration. Better yet are the museum's occasional one-hour praline-making courses – call for details.

MUSÉE DU COSTUME ET DE LA DENTELLE

☎ 02 213 44 50; Rue de la Violette 12; admission €3; ⏰ 10am-12.30pm & 1.30-5pm Mon, Tue, Thu & Fri, 2-5pm Sat & Sun; Ⓜ Gare Centrale; ♿

Lace-making has been one of Flanders' finest (and most eye-straining) crafts since the 16th century. While *kloskant* (bobbin lace) is believed to have originated in Bruges (see p109), *naaldkant* (needlepoint lace) developed in Italy but was predominantly made in Brussels. The Costume and Lace Museum reveals lace's applications for under- and outerwear over the centuries, as well as displaying other luxury textiles such as embroidery. Ask for an English-language booklet.

SCIENTASTIC MUSEUM

☎ 02 732 13 36; www.scientastic.com; Blvd Anspach, above premetro station Bourse; adult/concession €7.10/5.60; ⏰ 10.30am-5.30pm Mon, Tue, Thu & Fri, 2-5.30pm Wed, Sat & Sun; 🚇 Bourse

Kids aged six and over may yet think science is fun after a couple of hours at this interactive museum, where they can make their voice mimic a duck, 'fly' using mirrors and enjoy other sensory pursuits. A winner for rainy days.

🛍 SHOP

Pedestrianised Rue Neuve is wall-to-wall with high-street chain stores and elbow-to-elbow with shoppers on Saturday afternoons. The city centre also has some beautiful (and some very ordinary) covered arcades. Comic collectors will find plenty of treasures on the southern stretches of Blvd Anspach and Rue du Midi.

BOUTIQUE TINTIN *Comics*

☎ 02 514 51 52; Rue de la Colline 13; ⏰ 10am-6pm Mon-Sat, 11am-5pm Sun; Ⓜ Gare Centrale

No prizes for guessing the star of this comic shop, which stocks albums galore and cute merchandise.

🏠 CITY 2 *Shopping Mall*
Rue Neuve 123; Ⓜ Rogier
This modern shopping mall has all the usual chain-store suspects, but it's a good bet for electronic gear from FNAC, which also sells events tickets (see p169). In the mall's basement you'll find a post office, and a better-than-average food court – try Ganesh for fantastic Indian samosas, curries and naan breads.

🏠 DE BIERTEMPEL *Beer*
☎ 02 502 19 06; Rue du Marché aux Herbes 56; 🕐 9.30am-7pm; 🚇 premetro Bourse
As its name implies, this shop is a temple to beer, stocking upwards of 700 brews along with matching glasses.

🏠 DELVAUX *Accessories*
Galerie de la Reine 31; 🕐 10am-6.30pm Mon-Sat; Ⓜ Gare Centrale
Survey the gleaming handbags at Belgium's own Delvaux, established in 1829.

🏠 GALERIES ST-HUBERT
Shopping Arcade
off Rue du Marché aux Herbes; Ⓜ Gare Centrale
Opened in 1847, Europe's first-ever covered shopping gallery comprises three connecting arcades beneath its vaulted glass roof: Galerie du Roi, Galerie de la Reine and the smaller, perpendicular Galerie des Princes. Between them, the arcades contain a cinema, theatre, cafés and some wonderful shops selling chocolate, books and music, fashion and accessories (including Belgian Delvaux handbags, see review left).

🏠 NEUHAUS *Chocolate*
☎ 02 512 63 59; Galerie de la Reine 25; 🕐 10am-8pm Mon-Sat, 10am-7pm Sun; Ⓜ Gare Centrale
Framed by stained-glass windows, this is the original shop of the inventor of the praline, opened in 1857.

🏠 PASSAGE DU NORD
Shopping Arcade
off Rue Neuve; Ⓜ De Brouckère
Passage du Nord's array of quality boutiques makes this vaulted glass arcade a good spot to escape the rain.

🏠 PLANÈTE CHOCOLAT
Chocolate, Tearoom
☎ 02 511 07 55; www.planetechocolat .be; Rue du Lombard 24; 🕐 11am-6.30pm Tue-Sat; 🚇 premetro Bourse
You can catch praline-making demonstrations every Saturday at 4pm (€7) at this experimental chocolate shop famed for its chocolate floral 'bouquets' and other innovative shapes. If the

weather's behaving you can sip hot chocolate on the tearoom's outdoor terrace.

📖 STERLING BOOKS *Books*
☎ 02 223 62 23; Rue du Fossé aux Loups 38; ⏰ 10am-7pm Mon-Sat, noon-6.30pm Sun; Ⓜ De Brouckère

There's a fantastic selection of travel guides on the 1st floor of this friendly English-language bookshop, plus a good range of history and art books.

📖 WATERSTONES *Books*
☎ 02 219 27 08; Blvd Adolphe Max 71-75; ⏰ 9am-7pm Mon-Sat, 11.30am-6pm Sun; Ⓜ De Brouckère

This British emporium has Brussels' most comprehensive range of English-language books.

🍴 EAT

🍴 ARCADI *Bistro*   €
☎ 02 511 33 43; Rue d'Arenberg 1b; 7am-11pm; Ⓜ Gare Centrale

The jars of preserves, beautiful cakes and fruit tarts of this classic bistro entice plenty of locals, as do well-priced meals like layered eggplant and cheese, all served non-stop by courteous staff.

🍴 BRASSERIE DE LA ROUE D'OR *Belgian*   €€
☎ 02 514 25 54; Rue des Chapeliers 26; ⏰ noon-midnight, Aug-Jun; Ⓜ Gare Centrale

If you're hankering for hearty Belgian fare (rabbit, pigs' trotters and the like), follow the locals' lead and head to the 'Golden Wheel', where the décor is inspired by the city's surrealists.

🍴 DANDOY
Biscuiterie & Tearoom
☎ 02 512 65 88; www.biscuiterieda doy.be; Rue Charles Buls 14; ⏰ 9.30am-6.30pm Mon-Sat, 10.30am-6.30pm Sun; Ⓜ Gare Centrale

Established in 1829, Brussels' best-known biscuiterie has five

---

BRUSSELS' BISCUITS

Two very different biscuits are typical of Brussels. *Pain à la Grecque* is a long loaf rolled in sugar granules. Its literal translation 'Greek bread' is actually a corruption of the Dutch 'Brood Van de Gracht' meaning 'bread from the ditch', because Augustine monks from a long-gone Brussels abbey used to hand it out to the poor.

Spiced with cinnamon, nutmeg and cloves, gingerbread-style *speculaas* biscuits were traditionally eaten on St-Nicolas' fest day (December 6), the day Belgian kids receive their main Christmas presents.

Both kinds of biscuits are available year-round at **Dandoy** (above).

BRUSSELS

GRAND PLACE & ILÔT SACRÉ

local branches, this one with an attached tearoom. The chocolate for Dandoy's choc-dipped biscuits is handmade by Laurent Gerbaud (see interview p93).

🍴 KOKOB *Ethiopian* €€
☎ 02 511 19 50; www.kokob.be; Rue des Grands Carmes 10; 🕒 restaurant 6.30-11pm Mon, noon-3pm & 6.30-11.30pm Tue-Sun; bar 6.30pm-midnight Mon, 11am-midnight Tue-Thu & Sun, 11am-2am Fri & Sat, ; 🚇 premetro Annessens or Bourse

Meals at this airy Ethiopian bar/restaurant/cultural centre are based around small, shared dishes, like spiced eggplant or finely ground spinach and

cheese, spooned onto a central *injera* (pancake), with more pancakes provided for you to rip apart and use to scoop up your meal. If you order a pot of Ethiopian coffee (€8), be prepared to wait 15 minutes while the beans are roasted, and to be wired all night.

🍴 LA MAISON DU CYGNE
Belgian €€€
☎ 02 511 82 44; www.lamaisonducygne.be; Rue Charles Buls 2; 🕒 12.15-2pm & 7.15-10pm Mon-Fri, 7.15-10pm Sat; Ⓜ Gare Centrale

Try for a table overlooking the Grand Place in this refined 2nd-floor restaurant where you can dine on bank-breaking, but beautifully prepared Belgian classics. Service is appropriately fussy and the wine list outstanding. Budget diners after a taste of Louis XIV grandeur should try the 1st-floor Ommengang bar (noon to 2pm Monday to Friday), where lunch menus cost €18, including a half-bottle of water.

🍴 SEA GRILL *Seafood* €€€
☎ 02 227 91 25; Radisson SAS Royal Hotel Brussels, Rue du Fossé aux Loups 47; 🕒 noon-2pm & 7-10pm; Ⓜ De Brouckère

You'd be hard pressed to find a more unlikely setting for Brussels' finest seafood than deep inside this '80s ode to interior atrium elevators

EPICENTRAL EAT STREETS
Low-hanging awnings sparkling with fairy lights, oyster stands set up on the cobblestones and aproned waiters hustling for business cram the city centre's main eat street, narrow Rue des Bouchers, intersecting Galeries St-Hubert. Yes, this is tourist central, and due to the absence of any standouts, locals invariably steer clear. For a quick bite, you will find locals on nearby Rue du Marché aux Fromages. Although its name means 'cheese market', it's dubbed 'Pita Street' for the proliferation of pita outlets where you can order a brochette (kebab) or felafel pita to eat in or take away from noon to around 6am.

WAFFLE ON

A sure-fire way to tell natives from tourists is how they order waffles. Locals never consume these sweet snacks with whipped cream, chocolate or other elaborate toppings (except sometimes fruit). Instead, a Brussels waffle (p151) – a large, light rectangle with 20 'squares', usually eaten in tearooms and brasseries – is traditionally buttered and sprinkled only with icing sugar. The Liège waffle, sold at small stalls such as the popular Belgaufra chain, is rounder, heavier and much sweeter, with sugar already baked into the dough, hence there's no sugar on top. Both the Brussels and Liège varieties are served nationwide.

and muzak. But at the Michelin-starred Sea Grill restaurant, chef Yves Mattagne and his team create just that in the open kitchen. Try the Brittany lobster, crushed and extracted in an antique solid-silver lobster press (one of only four in the world) and prepared at your table.

☿ DRINK

You'll readily find everything from cosy old brown cafés to cool retro bars and Art Nouveau splendours in the city centre. Surprisingly, the grand cafés right on the Grand Place aren't (quite) as pricey as you might expect.

Brussels' gay scene centres on Rue Marché au Charbon.

☿ À LA BÉCASSE *Pub*

☎ 02 511 00 06; Rue de Tabora 11;
☼ 10am-1am Mon-Sat, 11am-midnight Sun; Ⓜ Gare Centrale
An elongated, time-worn interior and spirited regulars make this place perfect for a jug of lambic.

☿ À LA MORT SUBITE

Pub, Brasserie

☎ 02 513 13 18; www.alamortsubite .com; Rue Montagne aux Herbes Potagères 7; ☼ 11am-12.30am Mon-Sat, noon-midnight Sun; Ⓜ Gare Centrale
Floor-to-ceiling square columns with brass hat-racks, massive

The beer is to die for at À la Mort Subite

mirrors, varnished timber panelling and leather banquettes make this a sublime place to try the namesake Mort Subite (Sudden Death) gueuze. If this twice-fermented beer is too sour for your taste, order a *kriek* (cherry) or *framboise* (raspberry) version. Soak it up with old-school snacks like omelettes for under €10. See also Sudden Death below.

Y AU SOLEIL *Bar*
☎ 02 513 34 30; Rue du Marché au Charbon 86; ☼ 10.30am-late; ⓡ premetro Bourse
This old clothes shop has been converted into a shabby-chic bar with good beats and surprisingly inexpensive drinks given its status as a favourite for posers in shades.

Y FALSTAFF *Bar*
☎ 02 511 87 89; Rue Henri Maus 17; ☼ 10am-2am; ⓡ premetro Bourse
An Art Nouveau vision of mirrors and glass worth a visit for at least one drink.

Y FONTAINAS *Bar*
☎ 02 503 31 12; Rue Marché au Charbon 91; ☼ 10am-late Mon-Fri, 11am-late Sat & Sun; ⓡ premetro Bourse
The ripped black vinyl seats, '60s tables and light fittings, and cracked tiles of this ultratrendy bar provide the backdrop for locals reading newspapers by day, until the party cranks up again come nightfall.

Y GOUPIL LE FOL *Bar*
☎ 02 511 13 96; Rue de la Violette 22; ☼ 9pm-5am; Ⓜ Gare Centrale
You can't help falling in love, or just wishing you were, as you sip the house fruit liqueur in this romantic bar near the Grand Place. The nooks and crannies here are crammed with old records and paintings, and Brel et al croon in the background.

Y LE CIRIO *Bar*
☎ 02 512 13 95; Rue de la Bourse 18; ☼ 10am-1am; ⓡ premetro Bourse

---

SUDDEN DEATH
The alarming pub name À la Mort Subite (p51) dates from 1910 when National Bank of Belgium employees played a lunchtime card game of '421' at Theophile Vossen's neighbouring café, La Cour Royale. Before returning to work, their final fast and furious game was dubbed the *mort subite* (sudden death). When Theophile shifted to the café's current location in 1928, he named the new premises after this daily showdown. In turn, Mort Subite beer was named after the café. Today, the café and its exquisitely preserved original décor are overseen by the fourth generation of the Vossen family.

WRONG COFFEE

Belgium may brew beer brilliantly, but when it comes to coffee, it's no Italy. Cappuccino froth is frequently made from artificial whipped cream, and the closest thing you'll get to a latte is a *koffie verkeerd* (or *lait Russe* 'Russian milk' in French; the Dutch name literally translates as 'wrong coffee' since it has more milk than coffee). If you simply ask for 'coffee', you'll be brought a regular-size cup of black coffee (invariably called an espresso, regardless of the machinery used) with a tub of long-life milk and a small chocolate or biscuit.

Anything but off-the-tourist-track, but still a fixture for locals sipping the signature half-and-half (half wine, half champagne), this 1886 grand café could be a film set, with lots of dark timber, glass cabinets and lighting giving it a sepia-tinged glow.

⭐ PLAY

⭐ ACTOR'S STUDIO *Cinema*
☎ 02 512 16 96; Petite Rue des Bouchers 16; 🚇 premetro Bourse
This intimate three-screen cinema shows arthouse flicks and mainstream reruns, and has a tiny bar.

⭐ ANCIENNE BELGIQUE
Live Music
☎ 02 548 24 00; www.abconcerts.be; Blvd Anspach 110; 🚇 premetro Bourse
AB's two auditoriums host a great range of gigs, especially rock, with both international and home-grown bands. There's a good on-site bar/restaurant that opens from 6pm (bookings essential).

⭐ ARENBERG GALERIES
Cinema
☎ 02 512 80 63; www.arenberg.be, in Dutch & French; Galerie de la Reine 26, Galeries St-Hubert; 🅜 Gare Centrale
Inside Galeries St-Hubert (p48) this Art Deco beauty concentrates on foreign and arthouse films.

⭐ DUKE'S *Club*
☎ 02 639 14 00; www.dukes.be; Rue de l'Homme Chrétien; admission varies; 🕐 11.30pm-6am Thu-Sat; 🅜 Gare Centrale
Done out in outrageous kitsch (lots of velour) by Miguel Cancio Martins of Buddha Bar, Paris fame, this club inside the Royal Windsor Hôtel lures an over-30s crowd. Yes, that means '80s tracks play alongside more up-to-date tunes.

⭐ LE YOU *Club*
☎ 02 639 14 00; www.leyou.be; Rue Duquesnoy 18; admission Thu-Sat €10, Sun €6; 🕐 11pm-5am Thu, 11.30am-6am Fri & Sat, 8pm-2am Sun; 🅜 Gare Centrale

More than a pretty face, the Théâtre Royal de la Monnaie is the birthplace of Belgium

Somewhat mainstream, but in a sterling location just off the Grand Place, this vast club has a labyrinth of dance floors and chill-out rooms, and gay tea dances on Sundays.

⭐ MUSIC VILLAGE *Jazz*
☎ 02 513 13 45; www.themusicvillage .com; Rue des Pierres 50; admission €7.50-20, plus €2 temporary membership fee; 🚊 premetro Bourse
The doors of this pair of 17th-century houses open at 7.30pm (check the website for dates and book ahead). Concerts start an

hour later and feature everything from Cuban to Polish to Chilean jazz as well as New Orleans brass and swingin' Sinatra standards.

⭐ THÉÂTRE DU VAUDEVILLE *Theatre*
☎ 02 512 57 45; Galerie de la Reine 13-15, Galeries St-Hubert; Ⓜ Gare Centrale
Cabarets, concerts and various theatre productions take place at this old theatre within the Galeries St-Hubert. Programme leaflets are available in the foyer inside the arcade.

⭐ **THÉÂTRE NATIONAL** *Theatre*
☎ 02 203 41 55; www.theatrenational
.be, in French; Blvd Émile Jacqmain 111-
115; Ⓜ Rogier
By virtue of being a bilingual city,
the Belgian capital has not one
but two national theatres. This
spanking-new glass-fronted
theatre is the Francophone counterpart of the Flemish Koninklijke
Vlaamse Schouwburg (p98).

⭐ **THÉÂTRE ROYAL DE LA
MONNAIE/KONINKLIJKE
MUNTSCHOUWBURG**
Opera, Dance
☎ 02 229 13 72; Place de la Monnaie;
Ⓜ De Brouckère
Belgium was born when an opera
at this grand venue inspired the
1830 revolution (see p178). It

primarily mounts contemporary
dance, and classic and new operas.

⭐ **THÉÂTRE ROYAL DE TOONE**
Puppet Theatre
☎ 02 511 71 37; www.toone.be; Petite
Rue des Bouchers 21; admission €10;
🕑 8.30pm Thu-Sat & 4pm Sat, closed
Jan; Ⓜ Gare Centrale
Eight generations of the Toone
family have staged classic puppet
productions in the Bruxellois dialect at this endearing marionette
theatre, and it remains a highlight
of any visit to Brussels. Shows are
aimed at adults, but kids love them
too. Discounted tickets for children
and concession holders are available for €7, except on Friday and
Saturday nights. The attached bar
opens from noon to midnight.

>ROYAL QUARTER & SABLON

Rising to the southeast of the Grand Place, the majestic Royal quarter and Sablon sector takes in the sweep of the Palais Royal, the grandiose Palais de Justice and the Mont des Arts area, where Brussels' premier collection of museums are all a few footsteps from each other, housed in some of the city's most magnificent buildings. Among them are the Musées Royaux des Beaux-Arts, the Musée des Instruments de Musique and Musée BELvue (Belgium's national history museum), as well as BOZAR (also known as the Palais des Beaux-Arts cultural centre).

Antique shops, tearooms and chocolate boutiques, frequented by fur-coated *mesdames* and *messieurs* and their coiffed pooches, cluster around the Place du Grand Sablon. This elegant square has a splashing 18th-century fountain at its centre and hosts a high-end antiques market on weekends.

Adding to the area's rarefied air are graceful churches and the beautifully laid-out Parc de Bruxelles.

ROYAL QUARTER & SABLON

⊙ SEE
Cathédrale des Sts Michel
  & Gudule **1** E1
Église Notre Dame
  du Sablon **2** D4
Musée BELvue **3** E3
Musée d'Art Ancien......(see 4)
Musée d'Art Moderne...(see 4)
Musée René
  Magritte........................(see 4)
Musées Royaux des
  Beaux-Arts **4** D4
Palais de Justice **5** C6
Palais Royal **6** E4

Place du Petit Sablon **7** D5
Viewing Platform...........**8** C5

🏠 SHOP
Mary's...............................**9** F1
Pierre Marcolini............**10** C4
Sablon Antiques
  Market.......................**11** D4
Wittamer (shop) **12** D4

🍴 EAT
Le Perroquet.................**13** C4
Lola................................**14** D4

🍸 DRINK
Le Bier Circus................**15** F1
Wittamer (Pâtisserie
  & Tearoom)...............**16** D4

⭐ PLAY
BOZAR............................**17** E3
Musée du
  Cinéma **18** E3

Please see over for map

👁 SEE

On weekends, a single pass (available at museums; €11 for either Saturday or Sunday) covers the entire area of **Mont des Arts** (☎ 02 507 12 12; www.montdesarts.be), getting you into 15 different sights.

⏱ CATHÉDRALE DES STS MICHEL & GUDULE

www.cathedralestmichel.be; Place Sainte-Gudule; cathedral free, treasury museum or crypt €1, museum & crypt €2.50; ⏱ 8am-6pm; Ⓜ Gare Centrale
Rising out of a sea of 20th-century buildings, Brussels' twin-towered cathedral is named after Brussels' male and female patron saints. Construction began in 1226 but it would be another 300 years before it was completed, accounting for the hybrid of styles used – from Romanesque through to Renaissance. Take the stairs down to the crypt to see archaeological remains of an 11th-century Romanesque chapel.

🅒 ÉGLISE NOTRE DAME DU SABLON

☎ 02 511 57 41; Rue de la Régence 3b; ⏱ 9am-6pm Mon-Fri, 10am-6pm Sat & Sun; Ⓜ Porte de Namur
Built by a guild of crossbow enthusiasts at the start of the 14th century, this late-Gothic church sees sunlight streaming in through its stained-glass windows and on to its baroque chapels and intricately sculpted pulpit.

🅒 MUSÉE BELVUE

☎ 02 545 08 00; www.belvue.be; Place des Palais 7; adult/concession €3/2; ⏱ 10am-6pm Tue-Sun Jun-Sep, 10am-5pm Tue-Sun Oct-May; Ⓜ Parc; ♿
Inside this former royal residence, you can take a chronological audio-guided tour through Belgium's history from independence to today, brought to life by exhibits and snippets of film footage. In summer, the on-site restaurant sets up tables in the charming garden.

🅒 MUSÉE DES INSTRUMENTS DE MUSIQUE & OLD ENGLAND BUILDING

☎ 02 545 01 30; www.mim.fgov.be; Rue Montagne de la Cour 2; adult/concession €5/4; ⏱ 9.30am-5pm Tue-Fri, 10am-5pm Sat & Sun; Ⓜ Gare Centrale or Parc; ♿
Strap on a pair of headphones then step on the automated floor panels in front of the precious instruments (including world instruments and Adolphe Sax's inventions) to hear them being played. As much of a highlight as the Musical Instrument Museum itself, is its premises – the Art Nouveau Old England building. This former department store was built in 1899 by Paul Saintenoy and has a panoramic rooftop café and outdoor terrace.

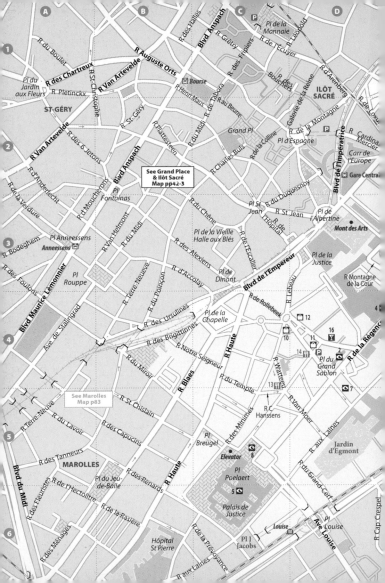

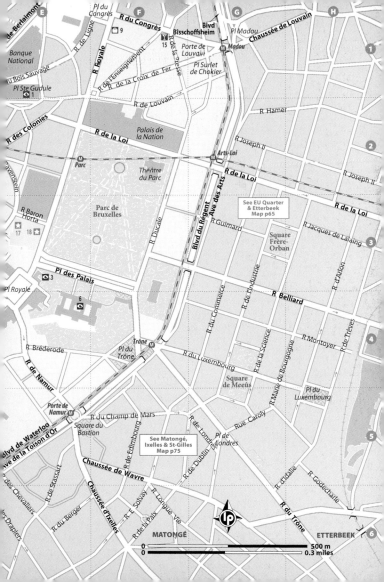

◎ MUSÉES ROYAUX DES BEAUX-ARTS

☎ 02 508 32 11; www.fine-arts-museum.be; Rue de la Régence 3; Musée d'Art Ancien adult/concession €5/3.50, Musée d'Art Moderne €5/3.50; ☼ 10am-5pm Tue-Sun; Ⓜ Gare Centrale or Parc; ♿
The country's most prestigious museums, the Royal Museums of Fine Arts incorporate both the Musée d'Art Ancien (ancient art) and the Musée d'Art Moderne (modern art). Among the many highlights are the collections of Flemish Primitives, the Breugels (especially Pieter the Elder) and Rubens in the Musée d'Art Ancien; and works by surrealist Paul Delvaux and fauvist Rik Wouters in the subterranean Musée d'Art Moderne. Also here as of early 2009 is the brand-new Musée René Magritte (see also below).

◎ PALAIS DE JUSTICE

☎ 02 508 64 10; Place Poelaert; admission free; ☼ 8am-5pm Mon-Fri; Ⓜ Louise

Impossible to miss (it's larger than St Peter's in Rome), this immense 1879-built law court was designed by Joseph Poelaert to reflect the temples of the Egyptian Pharaohs. There are sweeping views over Brussels from the viewing platform out front.

◎ PALAIS ROYAL

☎ 02 551 20 20; www.monarchy.be; Place des Palais; admission free; ☼ 10.30am-4.30pm Tue-Sun late Jul-early Sep; Ⓜ Parc; ♿
These days Belgium's royal family live at Laeken (see p91) but this 19th-century palace remains their 'official' residence, with unlikely décor such as a ceiling clad with the wings of millions of moths.

◎ PLACE DU PETIT SABLON

btwn Rue de la Régence & Rue aux Laines; ☒ 92, 93 or 94
This enchanting little garden is ringed by 48 bronze statuettes depicting the medieval guilds, and

RENÉ MAGRITTE

It's been a long time coming, but Belgium is finally honouring one of its seminal artists, René Magritte (1898–1967), by showcasing his works at the brand-new Musée René Magritte at the **Musées Royaux des Beaux-Arts** (above). Despite Magritte's mind-bending subject matter, such as a locomotive roaring out of a living-room mantelpiece in *Time Transfixed* (1939), for 24 years he painted in his bourgeois brick house in the Brussels suburb of Jette. If you fancy a trek out to the 'burbs, you can visit the house, open to the public as the **Musée Magritte** (☎ 02 428 26 26; www.magrittemuseum.be; Rue Esseghem 135; adult/concession €7/5; ☼ 10am-6pm Wed-Sun; Ⓜ Simonis then tram 19).

Primitive, surrealist, ancient, modern – the Musées Royaux des Beaux-Arts shed light on it all

offers respite in between sightseeing and shopping on the nearby Place du Grand Sablon.

SHOP

Rue des Minimes and its surrounding streets including Rues Charles Hanssens and Watteeu are lined with upmarket antiques shops. Some of the city's most exclusive chocolate boutiques are dotted around the Place du Grand Sablon.

MARY'S *Chocolate*
☎ 02 217 45 00; www.marychoc.com; Rue Royale 73; ⏰ 10am-6pm Mon-Sat; 🚊 92, 93 or 94

Established in 1919, and supplying Belgium's royal family with chocolates since 1942, Mary's is the grande dame of praline makers. All 70-plus varieties of all-natural chocolates (including scrumptious coffee creams) are created entirely by hand.

PIERRE MARCOLINI *Chocolate*
☎ 02 512 43 14; www.marcolini.be; Rue des Minimes 1; ⏰ 10am-7pm Sun-Thu, 10am-6pm Fri & Sat; 🚊 92, 93 or 94
Brussels-born Marcolini is the wunderkind of Belgian chocolate-makers, whose pralines include melt-in-your-mouth ganaches (cream-filled chocolate) made

INSIDER INFORMATION

Locals will tell you that Brussels is *une ville d'initiés*, meaning that to truly appreciate it, you 'have to know what's going on'. To find out, you can arrange a guided tour, dine in a private home or stay overnight with local residents. Bookings can be made through **Like a Local** (www.likealocal.com); prices depend on the activity. This scheme also operates in Antwerp. A similar scheme in Brussels is **Tof People** (www.brusselstofpeople.eu), which allows you to connect with hundreds of *tof* (Brussels slang for 'enthusiastic') inhabitants hailing from all over Europe. The service is free (excluding your personal expenses).

from exotic teas. Other Marcolini innovations include quirky bunny-eared Easter eggs. Make your selection from the glass counter then head to the back room to pick up your order. There's talk of a tea room opening soon upstairs.

🏛 SABLON ANTIQUES MARKET *Antiques Market*

www.sablonantiquesmarket.com; Place du Grand Sablon; ☎ 9am-6pm Sat, 9am-2pm Sun; 🚋 92, 93 or 94

Over one hundred vendors fill this stately square on weekends, selling crockery, crystal, jewellery, furniture, 18th-century Breton Faïence (pottery) and other relics of bygone eras. Prices generally reflect the high quality of goods for sale.

🏛 WITTAMER *Chocolate*

☎ 02 546 11 10; www.wittamer.com; Place du Grand Sablon 6; 🕙 Mon-Sat 10am-6pm, Sun 10am-6.30pm; 🚋 92, 93 or 94

The Wittamer family still makes its own excellent chocolates, which

you can buy at this boutique. They also run a pâtisserie and tearoom (see opposite).

🍴 EAT

Many of the museums in the Royal quater and Sablon also have excellent cafés/restaurants.

🍴 LE PERROQUET *Bistro* €

☎ 02 512 99 22; Rue Watteeu 31; 🕙 10am-1am; Ⓜ Porte de Namur

Perfect for a drink, but also good for a simple bite (salads, sandwiches etc), this Art Nouveau café with its stained glass and timber panelling is an atmospheric, inexpensive stop in an area that's light on such places.

🍴 LOLA *Brasserie* €€€

☎ 02 514 24 60; Place du Grand Sablon 33; 🕙 noon-3pm & 6.30-11.30pm Mon-Fri, noon-11.30pm Sat & Sun; 🚋 92, 93 or 94

Lola...yes, it's hard to get the Kinks out of your head at this streamlined contemporary brasserie. The menu is a combination of seasonal French and Italian (rack of lamb with thyme and onion *confit* and *dauphinois* potatoes, say), but it's the effervescent conversations of the young clientele bouncing off the stripped-back stone and wood surfaces that really gives this place its buzz.

DRINK

LE BIER CIRCUS *Beer Pub*
☎ 02 218 00 34; Rue de l'Enseignement 89; ⏰ noon-2.30pm Mon-Fri, 6pm-midnight; Ⓜ Madou
In a forgotten residential quarter of the city, you'll find beer connoisseurs debating the merits of Le Bier Circus' hundreds of brews.

WITTAMER
Pâtisserie & Tearoom
☎ 02 512 37 42; www.wittamer.com; Place du Grand Sablon 12-13; ⏰ 10am-6pm Tue-Fri, 9am-6pm Sat & Sun; 🚃 92, 93 or 94
Framed by candy-pink awnings, this exclusive pâtisserie and tearoom are part of the 1910-established Wittamer family's chocolate business, and a venerable Sablon tradition. You can buy the Wittamer family's chocolates at their nearby boutique (see opposite).

PLAY
Concerts often take place at the Cathédrale des Sts Michel & Gudule (p57), and at the Musée des Instruments de Musique (p57); check directly or with the tourist office for event details.

BOZAR
Concert Hall & Cultural Centre
☎ 02 507 82 15, bookings 02 507 82 00; www.bozar.be; Rue Ravenstein 23; Ⓜ Gare Centrale
Designed by Victor Horta in 1928, this Art Deco venue (formerly the Palais des Beaux-Arts) is the HQ of Belgium's National Orchestra and the Philharmonic Society, and is internationally renowned for its acoustics. It also hosts art exhibits.

MUSÉE DU CINÉMA *Cinema*
☎ 02 507 83 70; www.cinematheque .be, in Dutch & French; Rue Baron Horta 9; Ⓜ Gare Centrale
In a wing of the BOZAR cultural centre, Brussels' cinema museum is due to have reopened by the time you're reading this. You can browse through archives and memorabilia, but the real highlight are the silent films screened at its cinema, accompanied by a live pianist. Check the website for updates.

>EU QUARTER & ETTERBEEK

Visiting the EU quarter and Etterbeek reveals another of Brussels' many facets. When Brussels began headquartering European institutions in the mid-20th century, entire residential areas were flattened, giving way for the glinting glass, concrete and steel administration buildings that soar in their place today. Chief among these are the Berlaymont building with its four-winged exterior – constructed in 1967 and recently reopened as the home of the European Commission – and the architecturally uninspiring 1990s-built European Parliament, which redeems itself inside during a multilingual behind-the-scenes tour.

For all its functionality, the area retains graceful parks and squares, including the vast Parc du Cinquantenaire, and Parc Léopold, draped around duck-filled ponds. Flanking them are some stand-out museums showcasing all sorts from dinosaurs to automobiles.

The EU's expansion demands even more space, but development is more sympathetic these days. The neighbourhood is being unified with pedestrian and cycle paths, and is attracting residents once more.

EU QUARTER & ETTERBEEK

◉ SEE
Autoworld 1 E2
Berlaymont (European
  Commission) 2 D2
Chambres en Ville 3 A3
European Parliament 4 C3
European Parliament
  Visitor's Centre............5 C3
Musée des Sciences
  Naturelles...................6 C3
Musée Royale de l'Armée et
  d'Histoire Militaire......7 E2
Musées Royaux d'Art et
  d'Histoire....................8 E3
Square Marie-Louise......9 C1

◻ SHOP
Crush Wine 10 B3
Place Jourdan market ..11 D3

◫ EAT
L'Atelier Européen 12 D1
Maison Antoine 13 D3

▾ DRINK
Wild Geese 14 C1

★ PLAY
Arcade du Cinquantenaire
  drive-in 15 E2

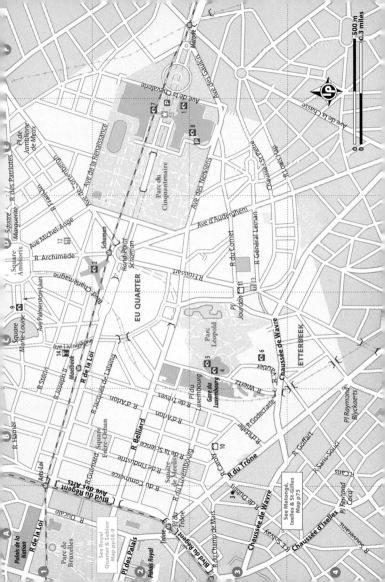

👁 SEE

👁 AUTOWORLD

☎ 02 736 41 65; www.autoworld.be; Parc du Cinquantenaire 11; adult/concession €6/4.70; 🕑 10am-6pm Apr-Sep, 10am-5pm Oct-Mar; Ⓜ Mérode; ♿

Prior to WWII, Belgium had a thriving auto industry and this coolest of car collections is its legacy. On display are some 400 vehicles (Model T Fords, Citroen 2CVs and much more, through to the 1970s), housed in a stunning 1880 steel structure.

👁 BERLAYMONT (EUROPEAN COMMISSION)

Rue de la Loi 200; Ⓜ Schuman

Although the 1967-built, star-shaped Berlaymont building that houses the European Commission isn't open to the public, the information panels outside give a succinct overview of the EU and its role in the European capital.

👁 EUROPEAN PARLIAMENT

☎ visitor's centre 02 284 34 57; www.europarl.europa.eu; Rue Wiertz 43; tours free; 🕑 tours 10am & 3pm Mon-Thu, 10am Fri; 🚌 38 (direction Homborch; departs from next to Gare Centrale) to De Meeus on Rue du Luxembourg; ♿

Inside this decidedly dated blue-glass building (completed only a decade ago) political junkies can sit in on a parliamentary session in the huge debating chamber known as the hemicycle, or tour it when parliament's not sitting. Tours (using multilingual headphones) start at the parliament's visitor's centre attached to the Paul-Henri Spaak section of the parliament.

👁 MUSÉE DES SCIENCES NATURELLES

☎ 02 627 42 38; www.naturalsciences.be; Rue Vautier 29; adult/concession/under 17 yr €7/6/4.50; 🕑 9.30am-4.45pm Tue-Fri, 10am-6pm Sat & Sun; Ⓜ Trône or Maelbeek; ♿

Colossal skeletons of iguanodon dinosaurs that roamed the land some 135 million years ago, found in a Belgian coal mine in 1878, are displayed in their 10m-high fossilised glory in this newly renovated and highly absorbing Museum of Natural Sciences.

👁 MUSÉES ROYAUX D'ART ET D'HISTOIRE

☎ 02 741 72 11; www.kmkg-mrah.be, in Dutch & French; Parc du Cinquantenaire 10; adult/concession €5/4; 🕑 9.30am-5pm Tue-Sun; Ⓜ Mérode; ♿

Antiquities and artefacts from non-European civilisations are the highlights of the Royal Museums of Art and History (including sections set up for the visually impaired), contrasted by comprehensive coverage of European decorative arts.

Kalina Lewanska
Communications, European Commission

Background? I moved to Brussels in 2003 to translate for the Commission. I'm from Poland and at first I was a 'curiosity' but since the EU enlargement I have more Polish colleagues. **Job?** Publishing scientific research on health and consumer protection issues affecting EU citizens like air quality, sun-bed radiation etc. My work covers the entire EU, so for meetings we need to find a common language – usually English, French or Italian. Outside work I'm a *tof* person (p62). **Best aspect of Brussels?** The multicultural atmosphere – for example, the African district (Matongé, p74) is a complete change to the EU quarter's coldness and bureaucracy. **Worst aspect?** The climate: things happen inside, not in the streets. **Will Belgium ever split?** Perhaps long-term. It would be a pity – Switzerland has different languages but works together as one country.

© MUSÉE ROYALE DE L'ARMÉE ET D'HISTOIRE MILITAIRE

☎ 02 737 78 11; www.klm-mra.be; Parc du Cinquantenaire 3; ⏰ 9am-noon & 1-4.45pm Tue-Sun; Ⓜ Mérode; ♿

One for military buffs, this museum houses an extensive array of weaponry, uniforms, vehicles, warships and documentation dating from the Middle Ages through to Belgian independence and the mid-20th century. There's a panoramic view of the park's triumphal arch (built in 1880), the Arcade du Cinquantenaire, from the top floor.

© SQUARE MARIE-LOUISE

off Ave Palmerston-Laan; Ⓜ Maelbeek

You can feed the ducks in this pretty tree-lined pond surrounded by greenery and a smattering of Art Nouveau architecture.

🛍 SHOP

🛍 CRUSH WINE Wine

☎ 02 502 66 97; www.crushwine.be; Rue Caroly 39; ⏰ 11am-7pm Mon-Fri plus 1 Sat per month; Ⓜ Trône

Brussels is too self-respecting to have a Fosters-spouting Aussie-theme bar, but international enough to have this wondrous cellar stocking over 190 Austral-

Take it outside at the Parc du Cinquantenaire (p64)

ian wines (the most comprehensive selection in Europe). Look out for rare drops from Tasmania and deliberate over dozens of Margaret River reds. There are daily tastings and tapas and regular wine events; call ahead for its schedule of Saturday openings.

🏠 PLACE JOURDAN MARKET
Market

Place Jourdan; 🕑 7am-2pm Sun
Ⓜ Schuman

Place Jourdan hosts a small Sunday morning market selling food and clothes.

🍴 EAT

This area is still something of a desert for dining (especially on weekends when most places close); Place du Luxembourg, Rue Archimède and Rue Franklin have the best pickings.

🍴 L'ATELIER EUROPÉEN
Belgian   €€

☎ 02 734 91 40; Rue Franklin 28;
🕑 noon-2.30pm & 7-10pm Mon-Fri;
Ⓜ Schuman

Fronted by a hedged courtyard, this former wine warehouse has a pared-down menu of meat and fish dishes such as sautéed veal and grilled sea bass, with a couple (but only a couple) of offerings for vegetarians. Wine is given its

> ### 'FRENCH' FRIES
> Just as the Brussels waffle originates from Ghent (p151), French fries hail from Belgium. The misnomer evolved during WWI in West Flanders, when English officers heard their Belgian counterparts speaking French while consuming fries (military orders were given in French, even to Dutch-only-speaking soldiers, with tragic consequences).
>
> Fries here are made from Belgian- or Netherlands-grown *bintje* potatoes. Hand-cut about 1cm thick – any smaller and they absorb too much oil and burn – they're cooked first at a lower temperature then again at a higher temperature to become crispy on the outside while remaining soft inside. There are dozens of sauces including the classic, mayonnaise.

due, with a well-chosen list and monthly specials.

🍴 MAISON ANTOINE *Fries*   €

Place Jourdan; 🕑 11.30am-1am Sun-Thu, 11.30am-2am Fri & Sat;
Ⓜ Schuman

Brussels can be divided into two kinds of people: not French and Dutch-speaking, nor locals and expats, but rather those who swear by this chip shop, and those who pledge allegiance to the caravan on Place Flagey (p81). Antoine's chips are twice-fried in beef fat and you'll see dignitaries and the odd celeb queuing for a coneful.

WORTH THE TRIP – ST-JOSSE & SCHAERBEEK

The residential quarters of St-Josse and Schaerbeek, northeast of the city centre, are little-explored by tourists, despite that the very-much-still-operating Gare du Nord train station makes this area one of the gateways to Brussels. Both neighbourhoods are home to Turkish and Moroccan communities, evidenced by the aromatic shops, restaurants and halal butchers you'll find here, such as along Chaussée de Haecht.

Also here are a trio of hip cultural spaces in historic settings. **Le Botanique** (☎ 02 218 79 35; www.botanique.be, in French; Rue Royale 236; M Botanique), on the edge of St-Josse, hosts Francophone theatre productions, exhibitions and concerts in an impressive neoclassical building from 1826. The building was originally the greenhouse of the city's botanic gardens, Jardin Botanique. Just north of Le Botanique is the **Halles de Schaerbeek** (☎ 02 218 21 07; www.halles.be; Rue Royale Ste-Marie 22; 🚋 92 or 93), a striking glass-and-steel former covered market hall built in 1901. This venue features circus arts, theatre, dance and opera plus contemporary concerts and multimedia installations. Heading east from Place Madou in St-Josse's southeast brings you to **Jazz Station** (☎ 02 733 13 78; www.jazzstation.be; Chaussée de Louvain 193a-195; 🕙 11am-7pm Wed & Sat & special events; M Madou). This temple to jazz hosts various concerts and exhibitions inside a disused 19th-century railway station. There is also a bar in the old ticket office.

For a drink or brasserie fare (like shrimps in white wine) in spectacular Art Nouveau surrounds, stop by **De Ultieme Hallucinatie** (☎ 02 217 06 14; www.ultiemehallucinatie .be; Rue Royale 31; 🕙 11am-1am Mon-Fri, 5.30pm-1am Sat; M Botanique). Built in 1850 in neoclassical style, this bar and restaurant was transformed in 1904 into the wrought-iron-filled showpiece it remains today. More Art Nouveau architecture is on show at the restored, 1893-built **Maison Autrique** (☎ 02 215 66 00; www.autrique.be; chaussée de Haecht 266; adult/senior/concession €6/4.50/3; 🕙 noon-6pm Wed-Sun; 🚋 92 or 93), Victor Horta's first creation.

Clued-in clubbers know the area for **Dirty Dancing@Mirano** (☎ 02 227 39 48; www .dirtydancing.be; Chaussée de Louvain 38; before/after midnight €5/10; 🕙 10.30pm-6am Sat; M Madou). DJs here include the likes of Cosy Mozzy and the atmosphere is electric. However, locals caution against walking through the poorly lit streets late at night and advise visitors to catch a taxi instead.

While this area is easily accessible by public transport, walking here from the EU quarter is a pleasant daytime alternative for those with a little more time. From Parc du Cinquan-tenaire, wander by the European Commission and north up Rue Archimède towards Square Ambriorix and the duck-filled Square Marie-Louise (p68). From here an easy stroll along Rue des Éburons and its continuation, Rue Willems, will take you through St-Josse. Continuing northwest brings you out at Jardin Botanique. Allowing for stops to take photos, or perhaps feed a duck or two, all-up this 3km walk should take about one hour.

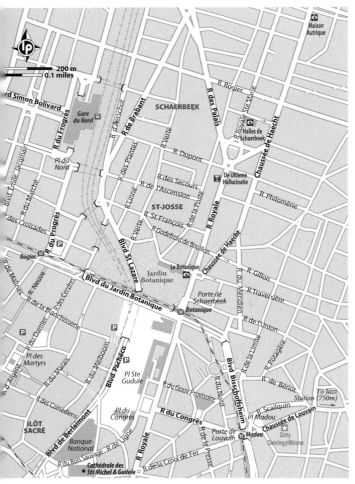

BRUSSELS

EU QUARTER & ETTERBEEK

Walk in the distinctive shadow of the Berlaymont building (p66)

🍸 DRINK

The EU quarter and Etterbeek empty out on weekends; check Place Jourdan for signs of life.

🍸 WILD GEESE Pub
☎ 02 230 19 90; www.wildgeese.be; Ave Livingstone 2; ⏰ 10am-late; Ⓜ Maelbeek

During the week, Eurocrats party like it's Paddy's day at Brussels' biggest Irish pub. It hosts regular live gigs, DJs and big-screen sports, and the kitchen turns out classic pub grub (loaded baked potatoes and juicy, thick-cut Irish steak), as well as a full Irish breakfast (OK, brunch – and with homemade soda bread!) from noon on weekends.

⭐ PLAY

Ask the tourist office for the programme of summertime drive-in movie screenings (with headphones available for non-drivers) under the Arcade du Cinquantenaire triumphal arch in the park of the same name. There are hip cultural centres and clubs in neighbouring St-Josse and Schaerbeek (p70).

>MATONGÉ, IXELLES & ST-GILLES

South of Brussels' historic centre, this trio of communities is a heady cocktail of sights, sounds, aromas and tastes.

You won't find Matongé (pronounced ma-tohn-*gay*) labelled on Belgian maps. Brussels' African district is informally named after an area of the Congolese capital, Kinshasa, and the vibrantly coloured fabrics, vegetables and spices spilling out of shops here indeed transport you to Europe's neighbour far south. Adjoining Matongé, hip brasseries and restaurants buzz around Rue St-Boniface.

Art Nouveau buildings grace the boulevards of Ixelles and St-Gilles, including Victor Horta's former home, which now houses the wonderful Musée Horta. Lined with luxury designer-label shops, swish Ave Louise cuts diagonally through Ixelles, leading to the city's university and fashion school, and the wooded Bois de la Cambre which adjoins the vast Forêt de Soignes. St-Gilles has an arty vibe in its upper town (though a rough, down-at-heel quarter in the lower town around Gare du Midi).

MATONGÉ, IXELLES & ST-GILLES

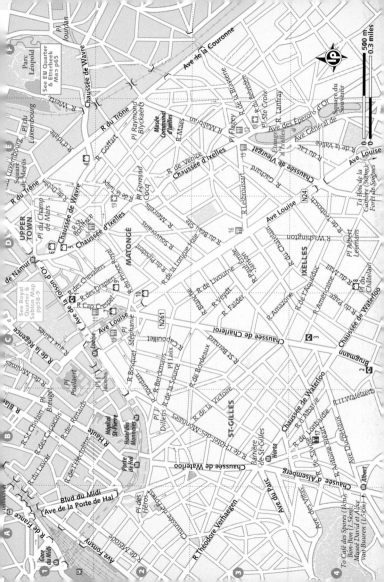

◉ SEE

◎ BOIS DE LA CAMBRE & FORÊT DE SOIGNES

🚊 93 or 94

A vast swathe of woodlands blankets Brussels' southeast. The Bois de la Cambre begins at the southern end of Ave Louise, and its lakeside lawns and cafés are filled with families on weekends. These woods neighbour the much larger Forêt de Soignes, a state-owned forest roamed by wild boar and deer.

◎ CITYSCAPE

Ave de la Toison d'Or; Ⓜ **Louise**
This enormous scrap-wood sculpture by Brussels artist Arne

Quinze is a whopping 40m-long, 25m-wide, 18m-high canopy that weighs more than 70 tonne. What it actually represents is anyone's guess. The adjacent open-air plaza hosts events during Brussels' tango festival (http://blog.brus selstangofestival.be) in April.

◎ HÔTEL HANNON & CONTRETYPE PHOTOGRAPHIC GALLERY

☎ 02 538 42 20; www.contretype.org; **Ave de la Jonction 1; admission €2.50;**
🕑 11am-6pm Wed-Fri, 1-6pm Sat & Sun;
🚊 91 or 92
If you're into photographic art you might want to catch an exhibition here. Even if you're not, it's worth

Don't knock it – the imposing Cityscape sculpture

WORTH THE TRIP – KONINKLIJK MUSEUM VOOR MIDDEN-AFRIKA/MUSÉE ROYAL DE L'AFRIQUE CENTRALE

Preserved insects, stuffed animals (including a huge elephant), masks, musical instruments, jewellery and a 22m-long pirogue (canoe) crafted by the Lengola people are among the mind-boggling displays at the extraordinary **Koninklijk Museum voor Midden-Afrika** (Royal Museum of Central Africa; ☎ 02 769 52 00; www.africamuseum.be; Leuvensesteenweg 13, Tervuren; 🚋 44; adult/concession €4/3; 🕙 10am-5pm Tue-Fri, 10am 6pm Sat & Sun; ♿), housing the world's largest collection of such artefacts outside Africa. Most artefacts were plundered during King Léopold II's exploitation of the Congo in the 19th century, something that is, finally, being increasingly addressed through the museum's displays. The on-site café serves African dishes, along with African beer, which you can walk off on the paths through the adjoining Park van Tervuren.

The museum makes a fascinating half-day trip, starting with the journey itself, on the old yellow tram 44 from its terminus at Montgoméry metro station, to the Dutch-speaking town of Tervuren (14km east of Brussels) along a tree-lined track. En route you pass stately embassies, the ponds at Parc de Woluwé and the northern tract of the Forêt des Soignes (opposite). It's an easy 300m walk from the Tervuren tram terminus to the museum.

stopping by for the splendid Art Nouveau building in which it's housed, Hôtel Hannon, designed in 1902 by Jules Brunfaut and graced by stone friezes and stained glass.

🖼 MUSÉE DAVID ET ALICE VAN BUUREN
☎ 02 343 48 51; www.museumvan buuren.com; Ave L Errera 41; adult/concession €10/5; 🕙 2-5.30pm Wed-Mon; 🚋 23 or 90

South of Ixelles in the wealthy residential enclave of Uccle, this Art Deco showpiece was built in 1928 by Dutch banker and art collector, David Van Buuren. Slip on the (supplied) plastic shoe cov-

erings to pad through the home, built from exotic materials such as ivory, to view paintings including a version of the *Fall of Icarus* by Pieter Breugel the Elder, and *Peeling Potatoes* by Vincent Van Gogh.

🖼 MUSÉE HORTA
☎ 02 543 04 90; www.hortamuseum .be; Rue Américaine 25; admission €7; 🕙 2-5.30pm Tue-Sun; 🚋 91 or 92

Although the exterior doesn't give much away, inside, Victor Horta's former home – which he designed and built between 1898 and 1901 and inhabited until 1919 – is an Art Nouveau jewel. Bathed in warm colours, the ground-floor living areas incorporate gleaming

TRAVELLING IN STYLE

Brussels' trams are undergoing a stylish makeover, with the addition of leather seats and large viewing windows, making them a great way to sightsee as well as get across town. This initiative of the City of Brussels is part of its drive to get cars off the streets and make the capital more eco-friendly. Eventually all of the city's trams will be replaced; refurbished trams that are currently up-and-running include 23 (Heysel–Gare du Midi), 24 (Schaerbeek–Vanderkindere) and 25 (Rogier–Boondael).

floor-to-ceiling tiling, while upstairs, you can see Horta's personalised touches (such as the nifty plumbed urinal behind a cupboard in the bedroom) in the small, intimate rooms. The lower level offers an overview of his work, including the scale model of his magnificent Maison du Peuple before it met with the wrecking ball (see also p160).

▢ SHOP

From the modern Galeries Louise shopping mall adjacent to the Louise metro station, stroll along tree-lined Ave Louise and its off-shoots for a fix of Cartier, Gucci and the like. Along Matongé's Chaussée de Wavre, grocery shops stock everything from catfish to dried caterpillars.

▢ **BEERMANIA** *Beer*
☎ 02 512 17 88; www.beermania.be; Chaussée de Wavre 174; ⊗ 11am-9pm Mon-Sat Jan-Nov, daily Dec; Ⓜ Porte de Namur or Trône
Staff have an encyclopaedic knowledge of the hundreds of beers available at Belgium's first-ever specialist beer shop and its on-site tasting café.

▢ **GALERIE D'IXELLES & GALERIE DE LA PORTE DE NAMUR** *Shopping Arcade*
Chaussée d'Ixelles; Ⓜ Porte de Namur
Bolts of African fabrics, Congo-lese CDs and hair salons doing braids and extensions fill these interconnected shopping arcades in Matongé.

▢ **MARCHÉ DU CHÂTELAIN** *Market*
Place du Châtelain; ⊗ 1-6pm Wed; ▢ 92 or 94
This gourmet food market brings trendy Bruxellois out in force. After you've finished shopping, hit one of the bars surrounding the square.

▢ **NICOLA'S BOOKSHOP** *Books*
☎ 02 513 94 00; www.nicolasbookshop .com; Rue de Stassart 106; ⊗ 11am-7pm Mon-Sat; Ⓜ Louise
Specialising in world literature translated into English, this welcoming independent bookshop

runs readings, author signings and poetry events. There's a small tearoom attached.

🏠 OLIVIER STRELLI *Fashion*
☎ 02 512 56 07; www.strelli.be; Ave Louise 72; 🕙 10am-6.30pm Mon-Sat; Ⓜ Louise

Congo-born Strelli is to Belgium what Georgio Armani is to Italy – an internationally renowned designer creating tailored men's and women's fashion that transitions seamlessly from the boardroom to cocktail parties and beyond. This light-filled boutique is Strelli's HQ.

🍴 EAT

🍴 BON-BON *Gastronomic* €€€
☎ 02 346 6615; www.bon-bon.be, in Dutch & French; Rue des Carmélites 93; 🕙 noon-2pm & 7-10pm Tue-Fri, 7-10.30pm Sat; 🚃 91 or 92

Brussels' most talked-about chef, Michelin-starred Christophe Hardiquest, shuns menus in favour of dishes crafted from the day's freshest ingredients from the markets. It's a bit of a hike out to residential Uccle, but for foodies this is as good as it gets.

🍴 CAFÉ DES SPORES *Belgian* €€
☎ 02 534 13 03; www.cafedesspores.be; Chaussée d'Alsemberg 103; 🕙 noon-2pm & 7pm-midnight Tue-Fri, 7pm-midnight Mon & Sat; 🚃 55 or 90

Getting here means trekking out to Uccle, but it's well worth it if you like chanterelles, porcini and other assorted fungi from the forest floor. Mushrooms feature in every dish (even the cep tiramisu) at this 'mushroom restaurant'. It sounds gimmicky but it isn't at all – the daily changing menu is market-fresh and there's a solid wine list.

🍴 COSPAIA *Gastronomic* €€€
☎ 02 513 03 03; www.cospaia.com; Rue Capitaine Crespel 1; 🕙 noon-2.30pm & 7-10.30pm Mon-Thu, noon-2.30pm & 7pm-midnight Fri, 7pm-midnight Sat, 7-10.30pm Sun; Ⓜ Louise

Cospaia's lush dining rooms done out entirely in glossy black and pure white are the work of Marcel Wolterinck, who designed singer Robbie Williams' London pad. Its menu (split equally between fish and meat) is sharp, stylish and very Brussels, right down to the desserts created by chocolatier Pierre Marcolini (see p61).

🍴 IL VECCHIO MULINO *Italian* €€
☎ 02 534 44 19; www.mulino.be; Rue Jourdan 10; 🕙 noon-3pm & 6-11.30pm; Ⓜ Louise

During Sunday lunch, this cosy restaurant feels like a communal dining room for the entire neighbourhood. But any time of the week it's a highly recommended option for authentic Italian pastas, meat and fish dishes, finished off with desserts such as chocolate tortes (platters are brought around to the tables for you to choose). Kids are warmly welcomed.

🍴 LE VARIÉTÉ *International* €€€
☎ 02 647 04 36; www.levarietes.be; Place Ste Croix 4; ⏱ noon-2.30pm & 6.30pm-midnight Mon-Sat, noon-11pm Sun; 🚃 81
Book ahead to take your seat in this Art Deco stunner in the Flagey building where you can watch the chefs preparing spit-roasted pork, chicken, beef and sea bass. Vegetarian options include wok-fried vegetables with mint and a heavenly goats cheese salad.

🍴 MAMMA ROMA *Pizza* €
☎ 02 640 42 80; Chaussée de Vleurgat 5; ⏱ noon-midnight; 🚃 81
For pizza *al taglio* (sold by weight) with toppings like pancetta,

pumpkin, walnuts and rocket, Mamma Roma hits the spot. You can take away or eat in, but it doesn't take reservations – just order at the bar (caveat: pickings are slim after 10.30pm).

🍴 ROUGE TOMATE
Mediterranean €€€
☎ 02 647 70 44; Ave Louise 190; ⏱ noon-2.30pm & 7-10.30pm Mon-Fri, 7-10.30pm Sat; 🚃 93 or 94
In a series of striking settings, including a light, white space and a decked courtyard garden, this hot address turns out fare from around the Med, such as a Moroccan vegetable tagine with tamarind and prunes, bull from the Camargue region of Provence, and rosemary-encrusted pigeon, with clementine sorbet for dessert.

🍸 DRINK
🍸 CAFÉ BELGA *Brasserie, Bar*
☎ 02 640 35 08; Place Flagey 18; ⏱ 8am-2am Sun-Thu, 8am-3am Fri & Sat, kitchen 9am-4pm; 🚃 81
DJs hit the decks on Friday nights at this Art Deco bar in the Flagey 'liner', with ad hoc music programming on other days, such as occasional Sunday jazz. The picture windows, deck-like interior and terrace all offer primo people-watching opportunities while you sip a Belga cocktail of vodka, Canada Dry and violet syrup.

AREA OF INTEREST – RUE ST-BONIFACE
The lively dining strip of Rue St-Boniface typifies 'new Brussels' with its multilingual clientele and diverse cuisines (traditional Belgian to Thai and more). For a good entrée to the scene here, start at the brasserie **L'Ultime Atome** (☎ 02 513 13 67; Rue St-Boniface 14; ⏱ noon-midnight; Ⓜ Porte de Namur).

AREA OF INTEREST – PLACE FLAGEY

When Bruxellois say something is 'hype', they don't mean overhyped but hipper-than-hip. Fitting that description is **Place Flagey** (🚊 81), a revitalised square near the Étangs d'Ixelles (Ixelles Ponds). The square's focal point is the restored, ocean-liner-like Flagey building, constructed in 1938 as the Belgian broadcasting flagship. It now houses a **concert venue** (below), a **cinema** (below), an international **restaurant** (opposite), and a fabulous **brasserie and bar** (opposite). On the square, the Frites Flagey caravan serves up what many consider to be Brussels' best fries. For amazing pizza, try **Mamma Roma** (opposite). A stroll south of the ponds will bring you to the leafy **Bois de la Cambre** (p76).

🍸 CHEZ MOEDER LAMBIC
Beer Pub

☎ 02 539 14 19; Rue de Savoie 68; 🕐 4pm-4am; 🚇 premetro Horta

An institution. Behind windows plastered with beer stickers, this tattered, quirky old brown café is the ultimate beer spot in Brussels. Sample some of their hundreds of brews while flipping through the collection of dog-eared comics.

⭐ PLAY

⭐ FLAGEY *Concert Hall*
☎ 02 641 10 20; www.flagey.be, in French; Place Ste-Croix; 🚊 81

A mixed but mainly contemporary programme of concerts take place in this former home of the National Radio Orchestra inside the Flagey building.

⭐ LOUISE GALLERY *Club*
☎ 0478 79 79 79; www.louisegallery .com; Galeries Louise shopping mall, Ave Louise; admission €11; 🕐 11pm-7am Fri-Sun; Ⓜ Louise

Buried inside the Galeries Louise shopping mall, this strobe-lit club has a wicked sound system that sees a diverse crowd dance till they drop.

⭐ SOUNDS JAZZ CLUB *Jazz*
☎ 02 512 92 50; Rue de la Tulipe 28; admission varies; 🕐 8pm-4am Mon-Sat; 🚌 54

In addition to local and visiting acts (especially experimental/contemporary), you can sometimes catch jam sessions here and always catch Sounds' good-time vibe.

⭐ STUDIO 5 *Cinema*
☎ 02 641 10 20; Place Ste Croix; 🚊 81

Located inside the Flagey building, this stylish new cinema spotlights various themes and directors.

>MAROLLES

The glass elevator from Place Poelaert, in front of the Palais de Justice, whisks you down the steep hill into what still seems like a different world.

Brussels' traditional working-class area, the Marolles, is known for its colourful dialect and its down-to-earth watering holes and markets. Although traces of these linger, the Marolles is prime real estate, wedged between the Gare du Midi, Ixelles and Sablon, a fact not lost on developers today. Nor was it lost on 19th-century architect Joseph Poelaert, who enlisted police to oust lifelong inhabitants of the area while building the Palais du Justice (hence the word *architekt* is a Marollien insult).

The Marolles is now home to gastronomic restaurants and nightlife. But to appreciate the area's roots, head to Place du Jeu-de-Balle early in the morning to see market traders setting up their stalls, and pop into one of the neighbouring bars for a hearty meal, strong beer and spirited conversation.

MAROLLES

⊙ SEE
Breugel House **1** D4
Église Notre Dame de la
  Chapelle **2** D3
Musée Bruxellois de la
  Gueuze
  (Cantillon Brewery).....**3** A3

⌂ SHOP
Gare du Midi market **4** B4
Halles des Tanneurs **5** C3

Place du Jeu-de-Balle
  Fleamarket **6** C4
Pêle Mêle **7** C2

⍥ EAT
Chéri Chéri **8** D3
Comme Chez Soi...........**9** C3
L'Idiot du
  Village **10** D3
Les Petits
  Oignons **11** D3

⍫ DRINK
Chez Marcel **12** C4
La Fleur en Papier
  Doré.........................**13** D3

★ PLAY
Bazaar 14 C4
Fuse 15 C5
Recyclart 16 C3

SEE

The free glass-elevator connecting Place Poelaert and the Marolles operates between 7am and 11pm daily, and gives you sweeping vistas over Brussels.

◉ BREUGEL HOUSE
☎ 02 513 89 40; Rue Haute 132; Ⓜ Louise

There is a museum in this step-gabled house where Pieter Breugel the Elder lived and died, but it's only open by reservation; phone ahead or check with the tourist office (p197) for details.

◉ ÉGLISE NOTRE DAME DE LA CHAPELLE
Place de la Chapelle; 🕑 9am-5pm Mon-Sat, 8am-7.30pm Sun; 🚇 premetro Anneessens

Built in 1134, this Romanesque Gothic church is Brussels' oldest and has a chapel devoted to Pieter Breugel the Elder who once lived nearby.

◉ MUSÉE BRUXELLOIS DE LA GUEUZE (CANTILLON BREWERY)
☎ 02 521 49 28; www.cantillon.be; Rue Gheude 56; admission €5; 🕑 8.30am-5pm Mon-Fri, 10am-5pm Sat; Ⓜ Gare du Midi

The real deal. This working brewery takes you behind the scenes of the production of gueuze – created by micro-organisms that cause the spontaneous fermentation of these unique lambic beers (see also p12). And of course, you get to taste it, too.

◉ WIELS
☎ 02 347 30 33; www.wiels.org; Ave Van Volxem 354; adult/concession/under 12 yr €6/4/free; 🕑 noon-7pm Wed & Thu, noon-10pm Fri, 11am-6pm Sat & Sun; 🚊 18 or 52; ♿

Brussels' old Art Deco Wielemans-Ceuppens brewery, just southeast of the Marolles, has been converted into a chilled new contemporary art space mounting six temporary exhibitions each year. You can leaf through art magazines at the café-

WHAT'S IN A NAME?
Brussels' bilingualism means that communes, streets, train stations and so on frequently (but not always) have two names, such as the commune of Elsene (Dutch) aka Ixelles (its French name). Street signs list the French, followed by the Dutch, such as 'Petite Rue de la Violette Korte Violetstraat' (Little Violet Street). In French, *Rue* (street) comes at the start, with the Dutch *straat* tacked on the end. Marolles signs contain three languages: French, Dutch and the Bruxellois dialect, resulting in mouthfuls like Rue Haute Hoogstraat Op d'Huugstroet ('High Street'). For simplicity, we've used the French names in this book.

Ground floor: the Marolles

restaurant and occasionally catch live music here.

🛍 SHOP

The Marolles' two main thoroughfares, Rue Haute and Rue Blaes, are prime hunting ground for retro homewares, bric-a-brac and vintage clothing.

🛍 GARE DU MIDI MARKET
Market

Gare du Midi; ⏱ 6am-1pm Sun; Ⓜ Gare du Midi
Said to be the biggest market in Europe, this sprawl of colourful stalls next to the railway lines has an international flavour, with exotic North African and Mediterranean spices, cheeses, meats, clothing, leather goods and everything else under the sun. Its food stands, selling bites like Moroccan crêpes with cheese, honey and vegetables along with mint tea, are a favourite with clubbers winding down from Saturday night.

🛍 HALLES DES TANNEURS
Books, Wine

☎ 02 548 70 40; www.hallesdes tanneurs.be; Rue des Tanneurs 60; 🚇 premetro Anneessens
To give you an idea where this neighbourhood's heading, stop by the Halles des Tanneurs, an Art Nouveau former tanning factory stunningly renovated to house a bookshop, wine shop and

designer florist, as well as a bar and restaurant.

⬛ PÊLE MÊLE *Books & Music*
☎ 02 548 78 00; Blvd Maurice Lemonnier 55; ☾ 10am-6.30pm Mon-Sat; Ⓜ Gare du Midi

You could lose yourself for hours among the shelves of this cavernous secondhand bookshop, which also stocks a vast array of CDs, comics and computer games.

⬛ PLACE DU JEU-DE-BALLE FLEA MARKET *Market*
Place du Jeu-de-Balle; ☾ 7am-2pm; Ⓜ Porte de Hal or premetro Lemonnier

The quintessential Marolles experience is haggling at this chaotic flea market, established in 1919. Weekends see it at its liveliest, but for the best bargains, head here early morning midweek.

🍴 EAT

🍴 CHÉRI CHÉRI *Bistro*   €€
☎ 025 200 89; Rue Haute 89; ☾ 8am-4pm Mon-Fri, 8am-6pm Sat & Sun; 🚇 premetro Anneessens

Carnival-like red, blue, green, yellow and orange striped walls, scrubbed floorboards and a stripped-concrete back room give this brand-new 'canteen' a casual-chic ambience. Smart bistro fare like risotto or gratin of endives is brought out on funky

crockery, and lopsided glass sugar bowls accompany your coffee, but service is pretty patchy. Still, it's early days.

🍴 COMME CHEZ SOI
Gastronomic   €€€
☎ 02 512 29 21; Place Rouppe 23; ☾ noon-2.15pm & 7-11pm Tue & Thu-Sat, 7-11pm Wed, closed mid-Dec to early Jan; 🚇 premetro Anneessens

The name evokes cooking just like 'at home', but unless you have a personal chef crafting the likes of North Sea lobster salad with black truffles and potatoes, sole fillets with Riesling and shrimp mousseline or perhaps spicy lacquered pigeon breast with wild rice, it's nothing of the sort. The prices are gobsmacking, but so is the food from master chef Pierre Wynants's son-in-law, Lionel Rigolet.

🍴 LES PETITS OIGNONS
Belgian   €€€
☎ 02 512 47 38; Rue Notre Seigneur 13; ☾ noon-2.30pm & 7-11pm Mon-Sat; Ⓜ Louise

Cosy up by the crackling open fire in winter or keep cool in the candlelit garden in summer at this Marolles mainstay. You'll need to exercise judgment when ordering the generous mains, as orders for dessert (including the house profiteroles) are taken at the beginning of a meal.

🍴 L'IDIOT DU VILLAGE
Belgian €€€

☎ 02 502 55 82; Rue Notre Seigneur 19; 🕒 noon-2pm & 7.30-11pm Mon-Fri; Ⓜ Louise

Booking ahead is essential to secure a table at this colourful, cosy place secluded on a little side street near the Place du Jeu-de-Balle flea market. Dishes are rich and aromatic (lots of herbs) and portions plentiful considering the cachet of this place.

🍸 DRINK

🍸 CHEZ MARCEL *Bar*

☎ 02 511 13 75; Place du Jeu-de-Balle 20; 🕒 7.30am-5pm; Ⓜ Porte de Hal

The more things change, the more they stay the same. This old-timer's bar is a bastion of the old Marolles spirit, serving up Cantillon gueuze, rib-sticking fare and atmosphere to spare.

🍸 LA FLEUR EN PAPIER DORÉ
Bar

☎ 02 511 16 59; Rue des Alexiens 53; 🕒 11am-midnight Mon-Thu & Sun, 11am-2am Fri & Sat; 🚇 premetro Anneessens

Artists adore this out-of-the-way Marolles bar where the walls actually do talk, in a sense, by way of the sketches and scribblings of the city's famed surrealists covering them.

⭐ PLAY

⭐ BAZAAR *Restaurant, Club*

☎ 02 511 26 00; www.bazaarresto.be; Rue des Capucins 63; 🕒 7.30pm-midnight Tue-Thu, 7.30pm-4am Fri & Sat; Ⓜ Porte de Hal

Upstairs, Bazaar is an over-the-top restaurant with flamboyant décor and international fare like ostrich in port wine (mains around €13 to €23). Downstairs, DJs spin rock, soul and funk in the vaulted former monastery cellar-turned-nightclub.

⭐ FUSE *Club*

☎ 02 511 97 89; www.fuse.be; Rue Blaes 208; before/after midnight €5/10; 🕒 11pm-7am Sat; Ⓜ Porte de Hal

Clubbers know this place as the home turf of megawatt DJs, like DJ Pierre, mixing house and deep house. Gay boys Europe-wide also know Fuse for its legendary La Démence parties (p170).

⭐ RECYCLART *Club, Art Space*

☎ 02 502 57 34; www.recyclart.be; Gare de la Chapelle, Rue des Ursulines 25; admission varies; 🚇 premetro Anneessens

This 'arts laboratory' in the Marolles' old Chapelle station along Rue des Ursulines revitalised what was once an industrial wasteland. It now hosts cutting-edge gigs and parties with DJs, art installations and theatre productions, and has a daytime café.

>STE-CATHERINE & ST-GÉRY

There's still a portside air in this eclectic inner-city neighbourhood. Brussels was once bisected by a network of waterways transporting goods, but the river and canals were covered over long ago to prevent disease, and for many years the area fell into disrepair. Its fortunes reversed again in the past couple of decades, and now Ste-Catherine and St-Géry are bywords for what's hippest and happening right now in the capital.

The main drag, Rue Antoine Dansaert, forms the focal point for Brussels' rapidly rising fashion scene, with avant-garde home-grown designers' boutiques, fabulous bars and a smorgasbord of places to dine. To Rue Antoine Dansaert's south, St-Géry has a pulsing nightlife scene; while to its north, Ste-Catherine overflows with seafood restaurants and open-air stalls.

Although gentrification continues apace, alongside the chic new establishments are narrow backstreets that still harbour old-fashioned shops, a world tour of ethnic groceries, and time-worn pubs patronised by salt-of-the-earth Bruxellois.

STE-CATHERINE & ST-GÉRY

◉ SEE
Église Ste-Catherine **1** C4
Zinneke **2** B5

🏠 SHOP
Christophe Coppens **3** B4
Hoet Design Store **4** B4
Le Bonheur **5** A3
Martin Margiela **6** B3
Natan XIII **7** B4
Nicolas Woit **8** B4
Stijl **9** B4

🍴 EAT
AM Sweet **10** C5
Comocomo **11** C5
Cremerie de
   Linkebeek **12** C4
Henri **13** B3
La Belle
   Maraîchère **14** C4
La Mer du Nord **15** C4
La Papaye Verte **16** C4
Le Pain Quotidien/
   Het Dagelijks Brood .. **17** C5
Viva M'Boma **18** C4

🍸 DRINK
Frederic Blondeel **19** C4
Le Greenwich **20** C5
Monk **21** C4
Walvis **22** A3

★ PLAY
Bizon 23 C5
Halles St-Géry 24 C5
Koninklijke Vlaamse
   Schouwburg 25 D2
L'Archiduc 26 C5

👁 SEE

👁 ÉGLISE STE-CATHERINE

Place Ste-Catherine; 🕐 **8.30am-5pm Mon-Sat, 8.30am-noon Sun;** Ⓜ **Ste-Catherine**

Built by Joseph Poelaert, who designed Brussels' Palais de Justice, the 19th-century Church of Ste-Catherine occupies the centre of this quarter. Its blackened façade is pretty scruffy, as is the open-air urinal against the western side, screened by a metallic forest-green fence.

👁 ZINNEKE

Cnr Rue des Chartreux & Rue du Vieux Marché aux Grains

In the old Bruxellois dialect, *zinneke* means 'a person of mixed origins', which sums up the city's inhabitants to this day. Hence Flemish sculptor Tom Frantzen's statue of a dog with its leg cocked is a proud mongrel, and has inspired the city's most exuberant celebration of Brussels' multifaceted make-up, the Zinneke parade (p26). For the full set of family snaps, stop by to see Manneken Pis (p44) and Jeanneke Pis (p44).

🛍 SHOP

Rue Antoine Dansaert is where it all happens. Wander along this strip and you'll find designer

Reflect on the latest fashions on Rue Antoine Dansaert

WORTH THE TRIP – THE ATOMIUM & BRUPARCK

Hop on the metro to the suburb of Heysel, north of the city, to reach Brussels' space-age symbol, the **Atomium** (☎ 02 475 47 77; www.atomium.be; Square Atomium; adult/concession/under 12 yr €9/7/free; ☼ 10am-6pm), just a few minutes walk from the station. Fresh from a facelift, this bizarre 102m-high stainless-steel structure was built for the 1958 World Fair and represents an iron molecule magnified 165 billion times. Its nine balls linked by columns are accessed inside by a series of precariously steep escalators and metal steps, and contain '50s furniture, various temporary exhibitions and a restaurant (due to reopen after renovations). Views extend across Brussels from the uppermost sphere. The whole thing glitters with sparkling lights after dusk.

Just across the road, the theme park, **Bruparck** (☎ 02 474 83 77; www.bruparck.com, in Dutch & French; Blvd du Centenaire 20), incorporates a water fun park, **Océade** (☎ 02 478 43 20; over/under 1.3m €15.50/12.50; ☼ 10am-9pm daily Jul & Aug, 10am-6pm Tue-Fri, 10am-9pm Sat & Sun Apr-Jun, 10am-6pm Wed-Sat, 10am-9pm Sat & Sun Sep-Dec & Feb-Mar, closed Jan), the giant Kinepolis cinema with a multiplex and an IMAX, and the highlight, **Mini-Europe** (☎ 02 478 13 13; www.minieurope.com; adult/under 12 yr €12.20/9.20; ☼ 9.30am-8pm Jul & Aug, 9.30am-6pm mid-Mar to Jun & Sep-early Jan, closed early Jan to mid-Mar). In the latter, over 350 miniature scale models (all 1:25) depict some of Europe's best-known architectural highlights, such as the cathedral of Santiago de Compostela (which took 24,000 man-hours to create), London's Big Ben, Lisbon's Torre de Belem and Paris' Pompidou Centre; with various moving features like little railways, and even a cross-section of the Chunnel. It's a fun way for kids (and kids-at-heart) to brush up on European geography, and the models are true works of art. On some weekend nights in summer Mini-Europe opens to midnight and has musical fireworks displays; call for dates.

Bruparck has plenty of fast-food outlets; otherwise pack a picnic and head to the leafy Parc de Laeken, which extends from the Atomium to the Domaine Royal, the residence of Belgium's royal family (closed to the public).

boutiques not only for fashion, but for funky accessories and homewares, such as the **Hoet Design Store** (Rue Antoine Dansaert 97) stocking Flemish-designed Theo eyewear, and **Natan XIII** (Rue Antoine Dansaert 101) run by local style-meister Thierry Struvay, with eye-catching window displays.

CHRISTOPHE COPPENS *Hats*
☎ 02 512 77 97; christophecoppens
.com; Rue Léon Lepage 2; ☼ 11am-6pm
Tue-Sat; Ⓜ Ste-Catherine
Coppens' head-turning creations have a dramatic flair, reflecting the fact that this Flemish milliner originally trained as a theatre designer and actor. This is his main

BRUSSELS

STE-CATHERINE & ST-GÉRY

womens' hat store; ask the helpful staff if you're looking for his men's, bridal or racing carnival headwear.

🎵 LE BONHEUR *Music & Films*
☎ 02 511 64 14; Rue Antoine Dansaert 196; ⏲ 11am-7pm Mon-Sat; Ⓜ Ste-Catherine

Located up the top, still-evolving end of Rue Antoine Dansaert, Le Bonheur is prime browsing territory for music ranging from electronica to world, plus short films and animations, with DJs sometimes spinning instore.

👕 MARTIN MARGIELA *Fashion*
☎ 02 223 75 20; www.martinmargiela .com; Rue de Flandre 114; ⏲ 11am-7pm Mon-Sat; Ⓜ Ste-Catherine

Margiela is often tagged the unofficial seventh member of the Antwerp Six (he graduated from Antwerp's fashion academy in 1980). Shoes, accessories, men's and women's body-skimming fashions in understated colours are artfully arranged in this white-on-white boutique.

👕 NICOLAS WOIT *Fashion*
☎ 02 503 48 32; www.nicolaswoit.com; Rue Antoine Dansaert 80; ⏲ 10.30am-1pm & 2-6pm Tue-Fri & Sun, 10.30am-6.30pm Sat; Ⓜ Ste-Catherine

Vintage fabrics found at flea markets and Barbie dolls from the '50s and '60s (such as the perma-tanned Hawaiian Barbie on display) are the inspiration for the fashions of this Brussels-born designer, who trained with Issey Miyake and Thierry Mugler in Paris.

👕 STIJL *Fashion*
☎ 02 512 03 13; Rue Antoine Dansaert 74; ⏲ 10.30am-6.30pm; Ⓜ Ste-Catherine

Brussels' top fashion showroom not only has labels by Belgian icons like Antwerp Sixers Ann Demeulemeester and Dries Van Noten, but also emerging new designers like Cathy Pill, whose atelier is just around the corner. Climb the wooden staircase at the back to the 1st floor to hunt for end-of-season bargains.

🍴 EAT

Place St-Catherine, Rue Antoine Dansaert and Quai aux Briques all excel for dining and are great places to trawl for a table. To really take the area's pulse, wander along Rue de Flandre, where a new wave of hip eateries sit cheek-by-jowl with old grocery stores and musty hardware shops.

🍴 AM SWEET *Tearoom, Sweet Shop*
☎ 02 513 51 31; Rue des Chartreux 4; ⏲ noon-6.30pm Tue, 9.30am-6.30pm Wed-Sat; Ⓜ Ste-Catherine

Laurent Gerbaud
Chocolatier

Background? My grandfather was a baker; I studied medieval history by day but chocolate-making at night, then did an apprenticeship before working in China, where my taste and ideas about chocolate changed completely. I started my company in 2001. **In what way did your ideas change?** I use no sugar, butter or alcohol. I work only with chocolate and play with salty, bitter and sour tastes like sweet chilli or Japanese citrus. **Business philosophy?** I source directly from the plantation and use only natural ingredients, no preservatives. Everything is handmade. It's a high-end niche market, like vintage wine – my chocolates cost €80 to €120 per kilo. Many chocolate companies are just about marketing but for me it's all about the quality. **Will Belgium ever split?** Everything will separate as if it was two countries, but we'll stay one country.

It's standing room only for fresh seafood at La Mer du Nord

Spiralling over two floors and several rooms, this charming *salon de thé/confiserie* on a village-like street resembles a Parisian apartment, with small metal tables, chairs in striped calico slip-covers, shelves of well-thumbed books, and framed watercolours resting against the walls. Not only is it a delightful spot for brunch or a fragrant tea, but the ground floor stocks an enticing array of sweets, including Laurent Gerbaud chocolates (see p93).

COMOCOMO *Basque Tapas* €
☎ 02 503 03 30; Rue Antoine Dansaert 19; ⏰ noon-3pm & 7-11pm; 🚇 premetro Bourse
At this much buzzed-about spot, *pintxos* (Basque tapas) such as

octopus or bite-sized ham sandwiches, glide past on an 80m-long sushi-train-style conveyor belt, and are colour-coded for easy identification (purple for pork, blue for fish and so on). But most diners' eyes remain fixed on the passing fashion parade outside the big picture-windows.

CREMERIE DE LINKEBEEK *Self-Catering* €
☎ 02 512 35 10; Rue du Vieux Marché aux Grains 4; ⏰ 9am-3pm Mon, 9am-6pm Tue-Sat; 🚇 Ste-Catherine
Brussels' best *fromagerie* was established in 1902 and retains its original glazed tiles. It still stocks a beguiling array of cheeses, which you can also try on crunchy ba-

guettes with fresh salad, wrapped in blue-and-white-striped paper ready to take to a nearby bench.

☝ HENRI *Belgian* €€
☎ 02 218 00 08; Rue de Flandre 113; 🕐 noon-2pm & 6-11pm Sat; Ⓜ Ste-Catherine
In an airy white space on this street to watch, Henri concocts tangy fusion dishes like tuna with ginger, soy and lime, artichokes with scampi, lime and olive tapenade, or Argentinean fillet steak in parsley. There's an astute wine list, and staff who know their stuff.

☝ LA BELLE MARAÎCHÈRE
Seafood €€€
☎ 02 512 97 59; Place Ste-Catherine 11a; 🕐 closed Wed & Thu; Ⓜ Ste-Catherine
Ste-Catherine has no shortage of superb seafood, but the wonderfully old-school La Belle Maraîchère has long been the restaurant of choice for discerning Bruxellois.

Here, the Devreker family reverently prepare lobster and fish, and it's the perfect place to try Brussels' famous mussels in white wine.

☝ LA MER DU NORD *Seafood* €
☎ 02 513 11 92; Rue Ste-Catherine 45; 🕐 shop 8am-6pm Tue Fri, 8am-5pm Sat, bar 8am-6pm Tue-Sun; Ⓜ Ste-Catherine
Beneath a cobalt-blue awning out on the pavement, fresh-from-the-ocean seafood including mussels, oysters and fish rests on beds of ice. You can buy some to take with you, or watch as it's cooked and snack standing up, accompanied by a glass of chilled Muscadet wine at the stainless-steel outdoor bar.

☝ LE PAIN QUOTIDIEN/ HET DAGELIJKS BROOD *Café* €
☎ 02 502 23 61; Rue Antoine Dansaert 16; 🕐 7.30am-7pm Mon-Sat, 7.30am-6pm Sun; 🚇 premetro Bourse
Now a successful multinational chain (p96), this is the original flagship of baker Alain Coumont, who launched his cafés here in

MUSSELS IN BRUSSELS
Steaming cast-iron pots of mussels (*mosselen* in Dutch, *moules* in French), appear on restaurant tables everywhere. They're traditionally cooked in white wine, with variations like *à la provençale* (with tomato) and *à la bière* (in beer and cream), and are accompanied by fries. Mussels were previously only eaten during months with an 'r' in their name, to be assured of their freshness, but modern cultivation techniques now mean mussels in July onwards are considered OK. Never eat any that haven't opened properly once they've been cooked. Beyond Brussels, mussels are also omnipresent in Bruges, Antwerp and Ghent.

STE-CATHERINE & ST-GÉRY

CHAIN REACTION

If you're looking for Starbucks, Burger King or KFC you're out of luck – Belgium doesn't have any. What's more, the country has the lowest number of McDonald's per capita in the developed world, and is the only nation where the golden arches aren't the number one burger chain. That honour goes to Belgium's home-grown (similar formula) version, Quick. Better still, Belgium pioneered the following ultra-healthy alternatives to fast-food outlets (locations are listed on the websites):

Exki (www.exki.be, in Dutch & French)
The Foodmaker (www.thefoodmaker.be)
Le Pain Quotidien/Het Dagelijks Brood (p95; The Daily Bread; www.painquotidien.com)

1990. Like its offspring, it revolves around a central wooden communal table, where local fashion designers, media types and post-clubbers rub shoulders over freshly baked bread and pastries, pies, salads and sandwiches, as well as sinful chocolate cakes.

🍴 LA PAPAYE VERTE
Vietnamese & Thai   €€
☎ 02 502 70 82; Rue Antoine Dansaert 53; ☺ noon-2.30pm Mon-Tue & Thu-Sat, 6-11pm Thu-Tue; 🚇 premetro Bourse
Wash down green and red curries, succulent noodles, and sizzling fried vegetables, seafood and meats with imported Thai beers at this busy yet relaxed southeast Asian restaurant. Service is prompt and the quality first-rate.

🍴 VIVA M'BOMA *Belgian*   €€
☎ 02 512 15 93; Rue de Flandre 17; ☺ lunch Mon-Sat, dinner Wed-Sat by reservation; Ⓜ Ste-Catherine

A white-tiled former *triperie* (offal butchers shop) now houses this fab restaurant. Viva M'Boma's name means 'long live the grandmother' in the old Bruxellois dialect, and the updated dishes here would make both Grandma and the departed butchers proud. Mains like veal kidneys, liver-based casseroles or horse steak are accompanied by hand-cut fries or *stoemp* (mashed potato), with *speculaas* (p49) ice cream for dessert.

🍸 DRINK

Ste-Catherine and St-Géry are crammed with cosy cafés and see-and-be-seen bars.

🍸 FREDERIC BLONDEEL
Tearoom, Chocolatier
☎ 02 502 21 31; www.frederic-blondeel .be; Quai aux Briques 24; ☺ 10.30am-6.30pm Mon-Sat, 1-6.30pm Sun; Ⓜ Ste-Catherine

The smart, minimalist interior of this Flemish chocolate-maker's premises makes it a stylish spot for a cup of tea while eyeing the elegant rows of pralines on display.

Y LE GREENWICH *Pub*

☎ 02 511 41 67; Rue des Chartreux 7; 🕑 10.30am-1am Mon-Thu, 10.30am-2am Fri & Sat; 🚇 premetro Bourse

Legendary as the den where Bobby Fischer and countless other chess masters have traded pieces, this brown café is still dominated by chess. Sitting and watching the players battling it out is entertainment enough

(which is to say there's no music, of course).

Y MONK *Pub*

☎ 02 503 08 80; Rue Ste Catherine 42; 🕑 4pm-2am Mon-Thu, 4pm-3am Fri-Sat; M Ste-Catherine

The Monk sprawls over two 17th-century rooms clad with timber and mirrors, and through not trying too hard, has become a regular hangout for with-it Bruxellois.

Y WALVIS *Bar*

☎ 02 219 95 32; www.cafewalvis.be; Rue Antoine Dansaert; 🕑 11am-2am Mon-Thu & Sun, 11am-4am Fri & Sat; M Ste-Catherine

Sounds from soul to punk to progressive rock (live, DJs or just through the speakers) play at this ubercool bar, where entry's free, the atmosphere buzzes and staff are great.

⭐ PLAY

Night owls will find plenty of action on and around Place St-Géry.

⭐ BIZON *Blues*

☎ 02 502 46 99; Rue du Pont de la Carpe 7; admission free; 🕑 6pm-late; 🚇 premetro Bourse

Not only a great place to catch new and classic blues, but something of a specialist beer pub and *jenever* café too.

WORTH THE TRIP – TOUR & TAXIS COMPLEX

Brussels' canal quarter has long languished, but the area (about 600m northwest of Yser metro station) is being given a new lease of life thanks to the regeneration of these old canalside warehouses and customs depots. Built over a century ago by the Tour et Taxis family, who founded Belgium's postal service, today the buildings are being transformed into the **Tour & Taxis complex** (☎ 02 420 60 69; www.tourtaxis.be; Rue Picard 3; M Yser), hosting temporary exhibitions (such as *Star Wars*), and harbouring a growing collection of industrial-chic shops, bars and restaurants. The renovations are part of an ambitious blueprint to rehabilitate the entire canal quarter.

BRUSSELS

STE-CATHERINE & ST-GÉRY

⭐ HALLES ST-GÉRY
Bar & Exhibition Space

☎ 0486 22 35 20; www.hallessaintgery
.be, in Dutch & French; Place St-Géry 1;
🕐 exhibitions 10am-6pm Mon-Sat, bar
10am-midnight Sun-Thu, 10am-3am Fri &
Sat; Ⓜ Ste-Catherine

Occupying a huge, tiered former
market hall on what was once an
island, Halles St-Géry has an enormous obelisk at its centre marking
'kilometre zero' – the point from
which all distances in Belgium
are measured. Halles St-Géry
now hosts art exhibitions by day,
and the bar cranks of an evening
when DJs spin funk, house and
more. In summer, the party spills
outdoors and goes on until the
wee hours.

⭐ KONINKLIJKE VLAAMSE
SCHOUWBURG *Theatre*

☎ 02 210 11 12; www.kvs.be; Rue de
Laeken 146; Ⓜ Yser

Behind a restored Renaissance
façade, the state-of-the-art Royal
Flemish Theatre mounts edgy
dance and theatre productions,
occasionally in English.

⭐ L'ARCHIDUC *Jazz*

☎ 02 512 06 52; www.archiduc.net;
Rue Antoine Dansaert 6; 🕐 4pm-late;
🚇 premetro Bourse

L'Archiduc is easily identified by
its jade-green façade. Ring the
bell to gain entry then lounge
with a martini in this 1930s Art
Deco bar, which has local line-ups
(free) on Saturday, international
acts (around €10) on Sunday and
a truly fabulous atmosphere. Gigs
start at 5pm.

Centuries old and still chiming – Bruges' Belfort (p101)

>BRUGES

To locals' bemusement, at least some of the city's 3.2 million annual visitors mistake it for an open-air museum, asking 'what time does Bruges close?'

True, Bruges' harmonious Gothic architecture, willow-lined waterways and market-filled squares are almost impossibly quaint. And the day-trippers crowded aboard canal boats and horse-drawn carriages clip-clopping through the cobbled centre do little to dispel the perception that Bruges' 700 year-old town gates are perhaps really turnstiles to enter this diorama.

But Bruges (Brugge in Dutch) is very much a living city, home to 117,000 people, including 20,000 within the moated historic centre. Beyond the souvenir shops you'll find cosy backstreet bars and cafés, young artisans and a palpable sense of history. Strolling Bruges' ancient streets early in the morning or after the last coach tour leaves reveals the city's soul.

BRUGES

☀ SEE

🏠 SHOP

🍴 EAT

Ⓨ DRINK

★ PLAY

Please see over for map

SEE

Bruges' tourist office (p197) sells various combination tickets, including a 'Combi-5' pass for five museums (€15), and a 'Cyclo-3' ticket for cyclists that includes entry to three museums and a free drink (€15).

BEGIJNHOF

Begijnhof 1; admission free, ⏱ 9am-6.30pm

Surrounded by protective walls, these whitewashed cottages – clustered around a central garden carpeted with daffodils in springtime – have an air of tranquil purity. Established as homes for a Catholic order of single and widowed women, there were around 1500 of these *begijnhoven* (or *beguinages*) in Belgium in the early 20th century, but only 22 remain. Dating from the 13th century, this is one of the best preserved, and home today to Benedictine nuns. The

tiny on-site **'t Begijnhuisje museum** (adult/concession/under 13 yr €2/1.50/free; ⏱ 9.30am-noon & 1.45-5pm Mon-Sat, 10.45am-noon & 1.45-5pm Sun) gives you an insight into a typical cottage. After your visit, prolong the serenity with a stroll in the swan filled Minnewater park nearby.

BELFORT

Markt; adult/concession/under 13 yr €5/4/free; ⏱ 9.30am-5pm

The symbol of Bruges is its Unesco-listed 13th-century belfry, rising a lofty 83m above the main square, Markt. Ascending the 366 steps brings you past the treasury, a triumphal bell and a 47-bell, manually operated carillon which still regularly chimes across the city.

BROUWERIJ DE HALVE MAAN (BREWERY)

☎ 050 33 26 97; www.halvemaan.be; Walplein 26; tours €5; ⏱ 45 min tours

IN BRUGES

Bruges hit the big screen when the 2008 Sundance Film Festival premiered the action-comedy, *In Bruges*. Written and directed by Irish playwright Martin McDonagh, the film stars Colin Farrell and Brendan Gleeson, who play two hit men ordered by their boss (Ralph Fiennes) to hide out in the city during the pre-Christmas frenzy. The tagline 'shoot first, sightsee later' gives you a fair idea of the success or otherwise of this outwardly benign mission – made more bizarre by their encounters with a string of surreal Felliniesque characters along the way. Various shopfronts were made over during filming, but the backdrop is quintessentially Bruges.

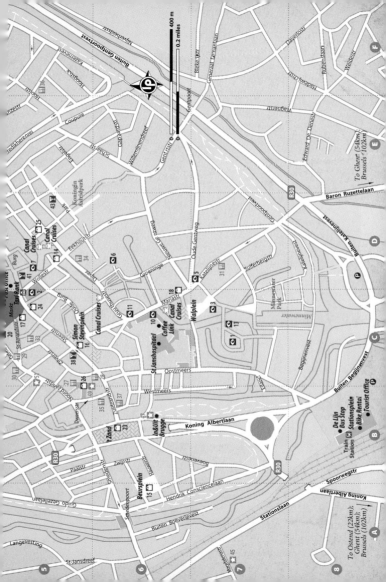

hourly 11am-4pm Apr-Sep, 11am & 3pm Oct-Mar; brasserie 10.30am-6pm, closed 2 weeks mid-Jan

This working brewery operated from 1856 until 2000 then was revived in 2005 by Xavier Vanneste (opposite), the sixth generation to brew here. Tours show you his family's historical brewing techniques and tools, which sit alongside the high-tech equipment he uses today to make blonde and double-brown Brugse Zot. As a reward for climbing the 'Half Moon' brewery's dozens of narrow steel steps, you get a fabulous view of Bruges' skyline from the rooftop, and a tasting at the end.

◉ DIAMANTMUSEUM

☎ 050 34 20 56; www.diamondmuseum .be; Katelijnestraat 43; museum only adult/under 12 yr €6/3, diamond-polishing show additional €3; ☽ 10.30am-5.30pm

Before Antwerp became Belgium's diamond capital, during the

Middle Ages that mantle was held by Bruges, as you'll discover at the city's diamond museum. Every day at 12.15pm, you can catch a diamond-polishing demonstration in the atmospheric medieval basement, but you'll need to arrive prior to noon.

◉ GROENINGEMUSEUM

Dijver 12; adult/concession/under 13 yr €8/6/free; ☽ 9.30am-5pm Tue-Sun; ♿

Highlights of Bruges' prized collection of art dating from the 14th to the 20th century are the Flemish Primitives (Room 2), including masterpieces by Jan Van Eyck and Hans Memling. But also look out for works by Hieronymus Bosch (Room 1), and surrealists René Magritte and Paul Delvaux (Room 9). Note that the museum will be partially closed in January 2009, and completely closed in February to March 2009; call the tourist office for information.

BURIED TREASURE

In the 1990s, when excavating for the foundations of the **Crowne Plaza Hotel** (Burg 10), workers literally hit a wall. This wall, it turned out, belonged to the 10th-century St-Donaas church (where Charles the Good, Count of Flanders is believed to have been assassinated in 1127), which later became a cathedral. Construction was allowed to proceed, provided that the remains were accessible to the public at no cost. It's occasionally closed for hotel conferences, but otherwise you're free to go down at any time (within reason) to find old maps, paintings, tombs and respite from the crowds above ground.

Xavier Vanneste
Managing Director/Brewer, Brouwerij de Halve Maan

Inspiration for relaunching the brewery (p101)? We'd made the museum but I wanted to go back to the roots and brew here again. **Why did it close previously?** A big brewing company bought it, then shut it down. Bruges once had 30 breweries and the same thing happened. We're the only brewery in Bruges' centre. **Annual production?** One million litres. Once, beer was for the poor people but now interest is rising, chefs are cooking with it. **Favourite restaurant cooking with beer?** Difficult question! Den Dyver (p112) really know what they're doing. **Favourite pub?** Again, difficult question! Brugs Beertje (p113) serves beer with knowledge. **Will Belgium ever split?** Not quickly. There are advantages and disadvantages. I don't know the solution to be honest. But it's manageable; there's no oppression, no war.

🅖 HEILIG-BLOEDBASILIEK

Burg 15; basilica free, museum adult/ under 12 yr €1.50/free; 🕙 **9.30am-noon & 2-6pm Apr-Sep, 10am-noon & 2-4pm Thu-Tue, 10am-noon Wed Oct-Mar;** ♿

Bruges' most treasured relic is a silver tabernacle containing the phial holding what's said to be a few drops of Christ's blood, hence the name of this 'Basilica of the Holy Blood'. The tabernacle resides in the 12th-century basilica's upper chapel, except on Ascension Day (approximately mid-May), when it's paraded through the city during the **Heilig-Bloedprocessie** (Holy Blood Procession; www.holyblood.com). You can see its jewel-encrusted reliquary used during the procession in the attached museum.

🅖 KANTCENTRUM

☎ **050 33 00 72; www.kantcentrum .com; Peperstraat 3a; adult/concession/ under 7 yr €2.50/1.50/free;** 🕙 **10am-noon & 2-6pm Mon-Fri, to 5pm Sat**

In the residential St-Anna quarter, Bruges' lace centre resides within a beautifully preserved almshouse. These terraced properties were built by merchant guilds for their members and by wealthy philanthropists for the poor and elderly. During the afternoon, you're welcome to watch informal gatherings of women making traditional bobbin lace in the small backroom. A small collection of traditional lace is displayed at the on-site museum.

🅖 MUSEUM ST JANSHOSPITAAL

Mariastraat 38; adult/concession/under 13 yr €8/6/free; 🕙 **hospital museum 9.30am-5pm Tue-Sun, apotheek 9.30-11.45am & 2-5pm Tue-Sun;** ♿

Six masterpieces by Flemish Primitive painter Hans Memling are the main draw of this chapel-turned-museum within Bruges' 12th-century St John's Hospital. These include the *Mystic Marriage of St Catherine* triptych (1479), along with works by other artists of the

---

MILLING AROUND

Ambling along the canal bounding the eastern side of the city takes you through pretty parkland past Bruges' four remaining windmills. From the 13th century through to the 19th century, Bruges' ramparts were graced with *molens* (windmills). You can visit two of the four, which still grind cereals into flour today, and which each house a little museum: the 18th-century **St Janshuismolen** (Kruisvest; adult/concession €2/1.50; 🕙 9.30am-12.30pm & 1.30-5pm Tue-Sun May-Sep), and the **Koeleweimolen** (Kruisvest; adult/concession €2/1.50; 🕙 9.30am-12.30pm & 1.30-5pm Tue-Sun Jul & Aug).

era. Admission is good for the restored 17th-century *apotheek* (pharmacy) next door.

⊙ ONZE LIEVE VROUWEKERK

Mariastraat; adult/concession/under 13 yr €2.50/2/free; 🕑 **9.30am-4.50pm Mon-Sat, 1.30-4.50pm Sun;** ♿
Flanked by a 118m-high tower, the 13th-century Welcome Church of Our Lady harbours some exceptional art, such as Michelangelo's marble *Madonna and Child* (1504), which was the only one of his works to leave Italy during his lifetime.

🛍 SHOP

Bruges has two main shopping streets. Steenstraat is where you'll find some international chains such as H&M, lots of shoe shops and a few department stores, interspersed with chocolate boutiques. One block parallel to the northwest is the much posher Noordzandstraat and its northern continuation Geldmuntstraat, home to designers such as Belgian Olivier Strelli, on the corner of Geldmuntstraat at Eiermarkt 3.

🛍 2BE *Artisan Products*

☎ **050 61 12 22; Wollestraat 43;** 🕑 **shop 10am-7pm, café noon-7pm**
Occupying a 15th-century Gothic mansion, this sleek emporium stocks a tantalising array of artisan chocolates, wines, *jenevers,* conserves, sweets, biscuits and other 100% Belgian goodies including a superb selection of beers, such as the local Brugse Zot, which you can try at the canalside café. Ask staff to fill you in on the escapades of the resident ghost of Perez de Malvenda, the former Spanish mayor whose house this mansion once was.

🛍 CHOCOLATE LINE *Chocolate*

☎ **050 34 10 90; www.thechocolateline .be; Simon Stevinplein 19;** 🕑 **10am-6pm**
Bruges has 50 chocolate shops, but just five where chocolates are handmade on the premises. Of those, the Chocolate Line is the brightest and best. Wildly experimental flavours by 'shock-o-latier' Dominique Persoone include bitter Coca-Cola, and black olive, tomato and basil; it also sells pots of chocolate body-paint (complete with a brush). Opening hours fluctuate.

🛍 DE REYGHERE REISBOEKHANDEL *Books*

☎ **050 49 12 29; Markt 13;** 🕑 **9.30am-12.30pm & 1.30-6pm Mon-Sat**
Poring over the huge range of travel guides in English, Dutch and French at this specialised travel bookshop is guaranteed to give you itchy feet. Its adjoining sister store has general nonfiction, novels and English newspapers.

WORTH THE TRIP – THE BELGIAN COAST

A quick train trip (or 50-minute bike ride) from Bruges brings you to Belgium's 65km of coastline (Map pp8–9). Despite its diminutive length, it's actually surprisingly diverse, with protected sand dunes and mud flats attracting migratory birds, and a string of beach resorts, each with its own character.

Highlights along the coast include the seafront promenade at the former glamour resort, now busy fishing port, **Ostend** (Oostende in Dutch, Ostende in French; www.inenuitoostende.be); *belle époque* **De Haan** (www.dehaan.be), Belgium's most captivating beach resort; highrise-dominated **Knokke** (www.knokke-heist.be), which hosts contemporary events including a photographic festival (April) and an International Cartoon Festival (June or July); the superb **Paul Delvaux Museum** (☎ 058 52 12 29; www.delvauxmuseum.com; Delvauxlaan 42; admission €5; ☒ 10.30am-5.30pm Tue-Sun Apr-Sep, Thu-Sun Oct-Dec, closed Jan-Mar) in St Idesbald, occupying the house and studio of Paul Delvaux (1897–1994), one of Belgium's most famous surrealist artists; and a cute theme park in De Panne, **Plopsaland** (☎ 058 42 02 02; www.plopsaland.be, in Dutch; De Pannelaan 68, Adinkerke-De Panne; adult/concession/child under 1m €23/22/free incl rides; ☒ 10am-5.30pm Apr-Jun, 10am-7pm Jul & Aug, 10am-5.30pm Wed, Sat & Sun Sep & Oct), which is based around Belgian TV characters like Plop the gnome.

Coastal trams (De Kusttram; ☎ 070 22 02 20; www.dekusttram.be, in Dutch) trundle almost the entire length of the coastline, stopping at all seaside towns and villages between Knokke to the northeast (near the Netherlands border), and De Panne in the southwest (near the French border). The entire strip takes just over two hours one-way, with 70 stops en route, including the towns listed above (and Plopsaland has its own tram stop). Trams depart every 15 minutes (from both Knokke and De Panne) from 5.30am to 11pm. A single ticket for a short/long journey costs €1.20/2, or you can buy a one-/three-day ticket for €5/10, which allows unlimited travel on the tram as well as local De Lijn buses.

Hourly trains connect Bruges with Knokke (€3, 15 minutes), Ostend (€3.30, 15 minutes), Zeebrugge (€2.40, 10 minutes) and De Panne (€7.40, one hour; change at Lichtervelde). The Coastal tram is linked with these stations either directly or by bus.

🎨 **DE STRIEP** Comics
☎ 050 33 71 12; Katelijnestraat 42;
☒ 10am-12.30pm & 1.30-7pm Tue-Sat,
2-6pm Sun
Look for Thibaut Vandorselaer's wonderful illustrated guides at this colourful comic shop. There's also a comprehensive collection in Dutch, French and English.

🎨 **ROMBAUX** Music
☎ 050 33 25 75; Mallebergplaats 13;
☒ 2-6.30pm Mon, 10am-12.30pm &
2-6.30pm Tue-Fri, 10am-6pm Sat

Here since 1920, this large, family-run music shop specialises in classical music, jazz, world music, folk and Flemish music, and is the kind of place where you can browse for hours.

'T APOSTOLIENTJE *Lace*
☎ 050 33 78 60; Balstraat 11;
🕑 9.30am-6pm Mon-Sat & 10am-1pm Sun
The garments and gifts at this lovely shop are made from beautiful and authentic lace handmade by two sisters and their mother; the husband of one of the sisters makes the wooden bobbins. See also right.

TINTIN SHOP *Comics & Gifts*
☎ 050 33 42 92; Steenstraat 3;
🕑 9.30am-6pm Mon-Sat, 11am-6pm Sun
Jigsaw puzzles, DVDs, figurines, T-shirts, albums and dozens of other items featuring Belgium's favourite cub reporter all cram the shelves here thanks to Bruges' 'Tintinologists'.

🍴 EAT
Locals are quick to warn visitors that restaurants gracing Bruges' beautiful Markt square are generally marketed towards tourists. As in any heavily touristed area, it's worth checking that your bill tallies up. If you want to dine with the locals, head just a few steps

back from the Markt. Alternatively, pick up some fries at either of the two *frietkotjes* (caravans) and grab a bench on the square.

Most of Bruges' eateries stop serving between lunch and dinner but you'll find a good selection of restaurants specialising in well-priced mussels (see also p95) along 't Zand overlooking the open-air plaza.

🍴 BAR CHOC *Café*   €€
☎ 050 61 15 44; www.bar-c.be;
Zilverpand 9; 🕑 11am-8.30pm
Hidden away in the Zilverpand shopping courtyard, this streamlined, contemporary café is chocoholic heaven, serving chocolate fondue, chocolate pancakes, rabbit in beer-and-chocolate sauce, as well as 44 different kinds of hot

STRAIGHT LACE
Although most lace (*kant* in Dutch, *dentelle* in French) sold in Bruges today is machine-made in Taiwan, it has been a traditional craft here since Charles V had it taught in convents. Duchess or bobbin lace *(kloskant)* is said to have originated in medieval Bruges, and you can still watch women meticulously manoeuvring delicate threads around pins using bobbins, following generations-old patterns, at the **Kantcentrum** (p106). To ensure you're buying the genuine locally made article, shop at **'t Apostolientje** (left).

Merchants of Bruges peddle their wares at markets throughout the city

BRUGES MARKETS

The charming squares and plazas of Bruges are picturesque settings for the city's numerous markets.

On Wednesday mornings, a rainbow of flowers and fresh food fill the Markt. Saturday mornings see produce piled up on 't Zand, along with clothes, baskets and other household items. Live chickens, rabbits, food and flowers are also sold on Saturday mornings on Beursplein. Fishmongers have been selling their North Sea catches for centuries at the colonnaded Vismarkt Tuesday to Saturday mornings; drop by for snacks such as *maatjes* (herring fillets). On weekend mornings, the Vismarkt area overflows with antiques and bric-a-brac.

and cold chocolate drinks (made from real chocolate, of course). The ginger hot choc – with bobbing pieces of handmade gingerbread – is wonderfully warming in winter.

CAFÉDRAAL *Seafood* €€
☎ 050 34 08 45; www.cafedraal.be, in Dutch & French; Zilverstraat 38; ☼ noon-3pm & 6-11pm Mon-Sat
Through a stone archway, this bistro/bar's hip yet homely multi-coloured rooms buzz with diners who come here for its outstanding bouillabaisse.

CHAGALL *Flemish* €€
☎ 050 33 61 12; St-Amandsstraat 40; ☼ closed Wed
Checked olive banquettes, candles, shelves cluttered with knick-knacks and an upright piano make you feel like you're dining in a family home. Seafood, such as several variations on eel, is Chagall's specialty, but it also does

daily meat specials and good deals on two- and three-course menus.

DA VINCI *Ice Cream* €
☎ 050 33 36 50; Geldmuntstraat 34; ☼ closed mid-Nov to Feb
Not being able to choose between the 40 luscious flavours of freshly made ice cream at this *gelateria* is a good thing, as it means you'll be offered small spoonfuls of free samples to help you decide (of course, that might just make the decision harder). Scoops cost just €1.20; in high summer it stays open until 11pm.

DE BRON *Vegetarian* €
☎ 050 33 45 26; Katelijnestraat 82; ☼ noon-2pm Tue-Sun; Ⓥ
Queues have usually formed by the time this glass-roofed restaurant's doors open, to get vegetarian fare direct from *de bron* (the source). Dishes are available in small, medium and large, and there are some delicious soups

such as pumpkin. Vegans are catered for on request.

🍴 DE KARMELIET
Gastronomic €€€
☎ 050 33 82 59; www.dekarmeliet.be; Langestraat 19; 🕑 noon-2pm & 7-9.30pm Tue-Sat, noon-2pm Sun
Chef Geert Van Hecke's intricate compositions such as Zeeland oysters, poached quail eggs, caviar and potato mousseline have earned him a trio of Michelin stars. The setting is slightly austere, but gourmands will be too busy swooning to notice. Lunch menus are a good deal, and Van Hecke is also in the process of opening a cheaper bistro. Book well ahead, especially for weekends.

🍴 DE STOVE *Belgian* €€
☎ 050 33 78 35; Kleine St-Amandsstraat 4; 🕑 lunch Sat-Tue, dinner Fri-Tue by reservation
Just 20 seats keep this gem intimate. Fish caught daily is the house speciality, but meat-based dishes on the monthly changing menu include the likes of wild boar fillet on oyster mushrooms. Everything, from the bread to the ice cream, is homemade.

🍴 DEN DYVER *Belgian* €€€
☎ 050 33 60 69; www.dyver.be; Dijver 5; 🕑 noon-2pm & 6.30-9pm Fri-Tue, 6.30-9pm Thu

Not only are the seasonal dishes at this elegant restaurant individually paired with beers, they're also cooked in Belgium's favourite nectar. One delicious example is the hare, turnip and cranberry ravioli cooked in Oude Gueuze, which is served with a Petrus Winterbier. Three-, four- and five-course menus can be ordered with a beer accompanying each course. There's also the option of pairing with wines, but that would be missing the point.

🍴 GRAN KAFFEE DE PASSAGE
Bistro €
☎ 050 34 02 32; www.passagebruges .com; Dweersstraat 26-28; 🕑 6-11pm
A mix of regulars and travellers staying at the adjoining hostel, Passage, give this candlelit, alternative Art Deco–styled bistro one of the best atmospheres in town. Its menu of hearty traditional dishes, such as *stoverij* (local meat in beer sauce) as well as filling tofu creations, is a bargain.

🍴 NIEUW MUSEUM *Flemish* €€
☎ 050 33 12 80; Hooistraat 42; 🕑 11am-2.30pm & 5.30pm-late Wed-Mon, 11am-2.30pm Tue
So called because of the museum-like collection of brewery plaques, money boxes and other mementos of café life adorning the walls, this family-owned local favourite

serves five kinds of *dagschotel* (dish of the day) for lunch (€7 to €12.50), and succulent meat cooked on a 17th-century open fire in the evenings.

¶ TOUS PARIS *Self-Catering* €
☎ 050 33 79 02; Zuidzandstraat 31; ⏱ closed Wed & Thu
If you and your arteries need a break from waffles and fries, this gourmet grocer offers a welcome alternative by way of fresh salads, quiches and made-to-order sandwiches on white or wholegrain baguettes.

¶ DRINK
Bruges has no shortage of beer pubs specialising in Belgium's finest drops. See p114 for drinking spots that also have live music and/or DJs.

¶ BRUGS BEERTJE *Beer Pub*
☎ 050 33 96 16; Kemelstraat 5; ⏱ 4pm-1am Thu-Mon
Legendary throughout Bruges, Belgium and beyond for its hundreds of Belgian brews, this cosy brown café is filled with old advertising posters and locals who are part of the furniture.

¶ CAFÉ VLISSINGHE *Pub*
☎ 050 34 37 37; Blekersstraat 2; ⏱ 11am-midnight Wed-Sat, 11am-7pm Sun

Luminaries have frequented Bruges' oldest pub since it first opened its doors in 1515. The interior is gorgeously preserved, but in summer the best seats are in the shady garden where you can play *boules* in between sips.

¶ CAMBRINUS *Beer Pub*
☎ 050 33 23 28; www.cambrinus.eu; Philipstockstraat 19; ⏱ 11am-11pm Sun-Thu, 11am-late Fri & Sat
Traditional Belgian and Italian-inspired snacks, as well as good-value lunch and dinner menus help soak up the hundreds of varieties of beer at this 17th-century sculpture-adorned brasserie/pub.

¶ DE GARRE *Beer Pub*
☎ 050 34 10 29; Garre 1; ⏱ noon-1am
This tiny beer-specialist pub packs 'em in for its exclusive Tripel de Garre beer. It's hidden in a narrow cul-de-sac between the Markt and the Burg and is notoriously hard to find; look for the gate on the side of the building.

¶ DE REPUBLIEK *Bar, Restaurant*
☎ 050 34 02 29; St-Jakobsstraat 36; ⏱ 11am-late
Set around a courtyard, this big, buzzing space is a favourite with Bruggelingen (Bruges locals), located in the same smart

premises as the art-house movie theatre, Cinema Lumière (right). DJs hit the decks on Friday and Saturday nights and there's also a great range of well-priced meals, including vegetarian options, available until midnight.

⛉ L'ESTAMINET *Pub*
☎ 050 33 09 16; Park 5; ⏰ 11.30am-late Tue-Sat, 4pm-late Sun, closed Mon
With its weighty dark-timber beams, low lighting, fabulous scratchy background jazz and convivial clatter, this neighbourhood café scarcely seems to have changed since it opened in 1900. It's primarily a drinking spot but also serves time-honoured dishes like spaghetti bolognaise with a baked cheese crust. Summer sees its loyal following flow onto the front terrace.

⛉ 'T POATERSGAT *Beer Pub*
Vlamingstraat 82; ⏰ 5pm-late
Look carefully for the concealed hole in the wall and follow the staircase down into this cross-vaulted cellar glowing with ethereal pure-white lights and flickering candles. Opened in 2007, 't Poatersgat (which translates from the local dialect as 'the Monk's Hole') has 120 Belgian beers on the menu, including a smashing selection of Trappists.

⭐ PLAY
Because Bruges' historic centre is residential, there are no nightclubs as such in town. The cafés and bars are the mainstay of Bruges' nightlife, and there are plenty of cultural happenings around town.

⭐ CACTUS MUZIEKCENTRUM *Live Music*
☎ 050 33 20 14; www.cactusmusic.be, in Dutch; Magdalenastraat 27
Though small, this is the city's top venue for contemporary and world music, both live bands and international DJs. It also organises festivals including July's **Cactus Music Festival** (www.cactusfestival.be), held in the Minnewater park at the southern edge of the old city.

⭐ CINEMA LUMIÈRE *Cinema*
☎ 050 34 34 65; www.lumiere.be, in Dutch & French; St-Jakobsstraat 36
Just a couple of blocks back from the Markt, this art-house cinema screens a well-chosen programme of foreign films in their original languages and is home to the Cinema Novo Film Festival (p26).

⭐ CONCERTGEBOUW *Concert Hall*
☎ 050 47 69 99; www.concertgebouw .be; 't Zand 34

The 21st-century notes of Bruges' Concertgebouw building

Bruges' stunning 21st-century concert hall is the work of architects Paul Robbrecht and Hilde Daem and takes its design cues from the city's three famous towers and red bricks. Theatre, classical music and dance are regularly staged. The tourist office is situated at street level.

⭐ DU PHARE Live Music
☎ 050 34 35 90; www.duphare.be; Sasplein 2; 🕐 kitchen 11.30am-3pm & 6pm-midnight, bar 11.30am-late, closed Tue

Tucked into the remains of one of Bruges' original town gates, this off-the-beaten-track tavern serves up huge portions of couscous (and offers free bread, a rarity in Belgium). But Du Phare is best known for its live blues/jazz sessions – check the website for dates. Bus 4 stops out the front.

⭐ JOEY'S CAFÉ Live Music
☎ 050 34 12 64; Zuidzandstraat 16A; 🕐 11.30am-late Mon-Sat

These days Joey's is run by Stevie, who performs with local band Cajun Moon and consequently, this dark, intimate bar is a gathering spot for Bruges' musos. You can sometimes catch live music here (call to check dates), or chill out with a creamy Stevie cocktail any time.

BRUGES

⭐ RETSIN'S LUCIFERNUM
Live Music

Twijnstraat 6-8; ⏰ 9pm-2am Sat
Behind the door of this private
home (ring the bell) lies an
otherworldly candlelit bar serving
potent rum cocktails and a live
band playing Latin American
music. Arrive early to get in.

⭐ WIJNBAR EST
Jazz

**☎ 050 33 38 39; Noordzandstraat 34;
⏰ 5pm-late Thu-Mon**
This wine bar is an especially lively
spot on Sunday nights when you
can catch live jazz, blues and
occasionally other musical styles
from 7.30pm.

>ANTWERP

Historic Grote Markt

>ANTWERP

Sexy, self-assured yet refreshingly unpretentious, Antwerp (Antwerpen in Dutch, Anvers in French) is at the forefront of 21st-century European style.

Harbouring medieval, Art Nouveau and adventurous new architecture, Belgium's second-biggest city is compact enough to see on foot, while comprising distinct quarters. The pedestrianised Meir shopping thoroughfare links the diamond district and Centraal Station with the historic core, which centres on the main square, Grote Markt. Just west of Grote

ANTWERP

Please see over for map

Markt, the fashion quarter showcases home-grown designers, while nearby, the revitalised 't Zuid (the South) is a cultural and nightlife hub. Undergoing gentrification is the 19th-century docklands, 't Eilandje.

Antwerp's trend-setting reputation builds on its long-standing tradition of creative industries, including Rubens' prolific studio of the early 1600s. Today this aesthetic flair extends to lighting and furniture and everywhere from hip clubs to hidden cafés, reinforcing the city's status as a barometer of cool.

🌙 SEE

Ask at attractions and museums about the various combination tickets on offer (one example being Antwerpen Zoo plus the Diamantmuseum). The city's churches, which contain an extraordinary cache of artworks between them, are closed to tourists during religious services.

🟢 ANTWERPEN ZOO
☎ 03 202 45 40; www.zooantwerpen.be, in Dutch & French; Koningin Astridplein 26; adult/concession/under 3 yr €16/10.90/free; 🕑 10am-7pm Jul-Aug, 10am-6pm May-Jun & Sep, 10am-5.30pm Mar-Apr & Oct, 10am-4.45pm Nov-Feb; 🚻
Home to over 6000 animals, including endangered species like the Congo peacock, Antwerp's zoo is believed to be the oldest in the world, yet conducts a progressive range of research programmes and has a planetarium.

🟢 AQUATOPIA
☎ 03 205 07 40; www.aquatopia.be; Koningin Astridplein 7; adult/concession €13.95/9.50; 🕑 10am-6pm

If you find yourself in Antwerp on a wet day with toey kids to entertain, this engaging marine theme park, with 10,000 fish in one million litres of water and lots of hands-on activities, will help assuage cries of 'I'm booored!'. Final entry is at 5pm.

🟢 DE ZWARTE PANTER
☎ 03 233 13 45; www.artsite.be/zwarte panter, in Dutch; Hoogstraat 70-74; admission varies; 🕑 1.30-6pm Thu-Sun & by appointment
Established in the heady days of 1968, the 'Black Panther' art gallery continues to redefine contemporary art through its exhibitions.

🟢 DIAMANTMUSEUM
☎ 03 202 48 90; www.diamant museum.be; Koningin Astridplein 19-23; adult/concession/under 12 yr €6/4/free; 🕑 10am-5.30pm Thu-Tue; 🚻
Try to time your visit to Antwerp's diamond museum for a weekday, when you can catch diamond-cutting demonstrations and an overview of the diamond industry's history and glitzy exhibits like diamond-studded jeans. There's

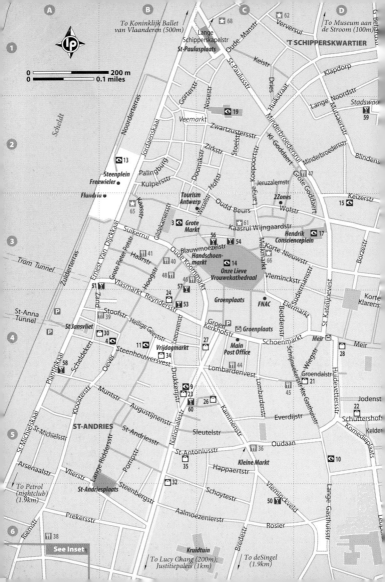

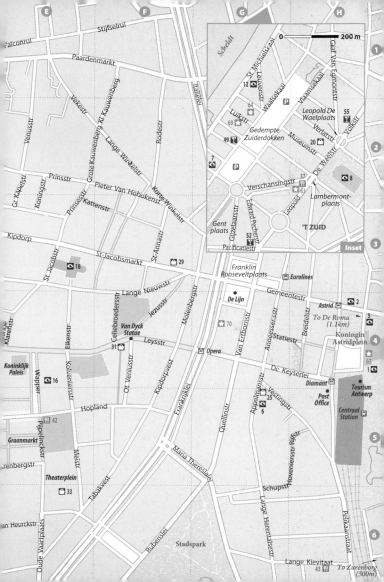

WORTH THE TRIP – ZURENBORG

To see Antwerp's finest examples of Art Nouveau architecture, hop on tram 8 or 11 or walk 30 minutes from Centraal Station to the peaceful residential quarter of Zurenborg in the city's southeast. Although none of the Art Nouveau buildings are open to the public, the flamboyant façades along Cogels-Osylei and its surrounding streets provide plenty of exterior photo ops. Detailed descriptions of architectural highlights are given in the tourist office brochures, *Zurenborg Walk* (€1.50) and *12 Adventures in Antwerp* (€3.50), but in any case the buildings are impossible to miss, thanks to their elaborate rooflines, wrought-iron balconies and detailing, such as stained glass and mosaics. Constructed mostly between 1894 and 1914, these showpieces were saved from demolition in the 1960s following protests by the community and artists throughout Belgium and beyond. All of the streets highlighted on the map below are rich with architectural treasures.

After strolling the streets, head to one of the inexpensive, atmospheric cafés and restaurants ringing the village-like square of Dageraadplaats, or try our pick for Belgium's best fries (handcut and fried in palm-oil), as well as Moroccan and Middle Eastern–inspired bites like spicy falafels at the funky little eat-in snack bar, **Frituur 't Spieke** (☎ 03 218 71 69; Klein Beerstraat 18; 🕑 11.30am-midnight).

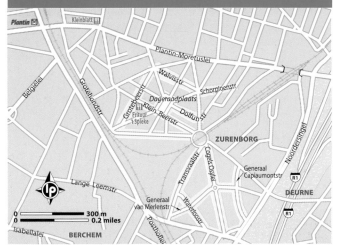

a special 'touch route' for visually impaired visitors.

◎ DIAMONDLAND

☎ 03 229 29 90; www.diamondland.be; Appelmansstraat 33a; admission free; ⏰ 9.30am-5.30pm Mon-Sat year-round & 10am-5pm Sun Apr-Oct

If diamonds are beyond your budget, you can watch them being cut and set during daily shows at 11am at this vast 1000-sq-metre diamond-showroom. If they're not, this is one of the verified sales points of the **Antwerp Diamond Jewellers Association** (ADJA; www.adja.be), which oversees quality control.

◎ FOTOMUSEUM

☎ 03 242 93 00; www.fotomuseum.be, in Dutch; Waalsekaai 47; adult/concession €6/4; ⏰ 10am-6pm Tue-Sun; ♿

The highlight of Antwerp's state-of-the-art photographic museum is the multimedia room tying together photography with film and new technologies, giving you a glimpse into the future of the genre. The kitchen of the stunning black-and-white café (also closed Mondays) stays open until 10pm.

◎ KONINKLIJK MUSEUM VOOR SCHONE KUNSTEN (KMSKA)

☎ 03 238 78 09; www.kmska.be; Leopold De Waelplaats; adult/concession/ under 19 yr €6/4/free; ⏰ 10am-5pm Tue-Sat, 10am-6pm Sun; ♿

Jan Van Eyck, the Breugels, Rubens, Van Dyck, Margritte and Delvaux are among the masters whose works are gloriously displayed against backdrops such as vivid crimson walls, at Antwerp's Royal Museum of Fine Arts.

◎ MODE MUSEUM (MOMU)

☎ 03 470 27 70; www.momu.be; Nationalestraat 28; adult/concession/ under 12 yr €7/5/free; ⏰ 10am-6pm Tue-Wed & Fri-Sun, 10am-9pm Thu; ♿

Antwerp's fashion museum is housed inside the light-filled **ModeNatie** (www.modenatie.com), along with the Flanders Fashion Institute and the fashion department of the Royal Academy of Fine Arts. The museum has no permanent

POTTING MIX

Digging through the website of **Pot-aarde** (Potting Mix; www.potaarde.be/ redactie) unearths unique perspectives of Antwerp as seen through the lenses of photographers involved in the Potaarde project. Each week, this accomplished group of snappers undertake a one-day mission to capture an aspect or theme of city life, such as *onder een brug* (under the bridge) or *leef nu* (living now). The diverse results provide a social commentary while illuminating little-known facets of the city.

The ultimate twinset – exhibit at Mode Museum (p123)

collection; instead, up-to-the-minute exhibitions rotate on a biannual fashion-show cycle.

MUSEUM MAYER VAN DEN BERGH

☎ 03 232 42 37; http://museum
.antwerpen.be/mayervandenbergh;
Lange Gasthuisstraat 19; adult/concession/under 19 yr & over 65 yr €4/3/free;
🕑 10am-5pm Tue-Sun
This jewel of a museum, inside a 1904 townhouse built in 16th-century style, contains an astonishing collection of over 3000 artworks amassed by collector Fritz Mayer Van Den Bergh. Unlike at larger museums, here works by Pieter Breugel the Elder, Flemish Primitives and late Gothic sculptures are arranged in small, intimate rooms.

MUSEUM PLANTIN-MORETUS

☎ 03 21 14 50; http://museum.antwer
pen.be/plantin_Moretus; Vrijdagmarkt
22-23; adult/concession/under 19 yr
& over 65 yr €6/4/free; 🕑 10am-5pm
Tue-Sun; ♿

While the world's oldest, Unesco-listed printing presses and rare books (including a Gutenberg bible) provide a comprehensive overview of book publishing between the 15th and 18th century, the original tapestries, leather-upholstered walls and rich artworks evoke how the printing masters lived. The ground floor has wheelchair access.

☉ MUSEUM VAN HEDENDAAGSE KUNST ANTWERPEN (MUHKA)

☎ 03 260 99 99; www.muhka.be; Leuvenstraat 32; adult/concession/under 13 yr €5/3/free; ☺ 10am-5pm Tue-Sun; ♿

Contemporary art from 1970 to today provokes and sometimes shocks in this converted grain silo and warehouse in 't Zuid. Alongside permanent collections, the museum has four major temporary exhibitions featuring local and international artists each year.

LAW UNTO ITSELF

The city's most arresting piece of architecture is its **Justitiepaleis** (law court; Bolivarplaats), which opened in 't Zuid in 2005. Locals quickly dubbed it the *frietzak* meaning 'cone of fries' thanks to its asymmetrical triangular glass roofline. It's the work of British architect Richard Rogers, whose résumé includes equally controversial buildings like Paris' Pompidou Centre.

☉ NATIONAAL SCHEEPVAARTMUSEUM STEEN

☎ 03 201 93 40; http://museum.antwerpen.be/scheepvaartmuseum; Steenplein 1; adult/concession/under 19 yr & over 65 yr €4/3/free; ☺ 10am-5pm Tue-Sun; ♿

Inside Antwerp's hulking fortress, the Steen (c 1200), you can explore the extensive collection of model ships, navigation instruments and other seafaring paraphernalia charting Belgium's maritime history. Outside, original ships, including a 1920s barge often used as an exhibition venue, are moored in the 'maritime park'. There's wheelchair access to the Steen's ground and 1st floors, and to the maritime park.

☉ ONZE LIEVE VROUWEKATHEDRAAL

Handschoenmarkt; adult/under 12 yr €4/free; ☺ 10am-5pm Mon-Fri, 10am-3pm Sat, 1-4pm Sun; ♿

The centrepiece of Antwerp's historic centre is the Cathedral of Our Lady, Belgium's largest and most ornate Gothic cathedral, whose lacy 123m-high stone spire is visible throughout the city. Built between 1352 and 1521, the interior is mostly baroque, and contains four of Rubens' early canvases: *Assumption*, *The Raising of the Cross*, *Resurrection* and the most famous, *The Descent from the Cross*.

🅞 ROCKOXHUIS

☎ 03 201 92 50; www.rockoxhuis.be; Keizerstraat 10-12; adult/concession/under 12 yr €2.50/1.25/free; ☾ 10am-5pm Tue-Sun; ♿

The collections of 17th-century mayor Nicolaas Rockox form the basis of this museum in Rockox' former home. Treasures include works by Van Dyck, Breughel the Younger and Rockox' chum, Rubens, among other masters.

🅞 RUBENSHUIS

☎ 03 201 15 55; http://museum.antwerpen.be/rubenshuis; Wapper 9-11; adult/concession/under 19 yr & over 65 yr €6/4/free; ☾ 10am-5pm Tue-Sun; ♿

Entering Rubens' painstakingly restored home through its inner courtyard, flanked by a baroque portico leading to Renaissance gardens that Rubens designed, creates the impression of stepping inside an Italian palazzo. Ten of his canvases are on display, including his definitive *Self-portrait*, and *Adam and Eve in Paradise*. Wheelchair access is possible to the garden and ground floor only.

🅞 ST-CAROLUS BORROMEUSKERK

☎ 03 231 37 51; Hendrik Conscienceplein 6; admission free; ☾ 10am-12.30pm & 2-5pm Mon-Fri, 10am-12.30pm & 2-7pm Sat; ♿

Tucked away on a charming square, this beautiful baroque church was completed in 1621. Rubens designed the façade, tower and decorative sculptures, though sadly an 18th-century fire destroyed dozens of paintings produced by the master and his studio.

🅞 ST-JACOBSKERK

☎ 03 232 10 32; Lange Nieuwstraat 73-75; adult/under 12 yr €2/free; ☾ 2-5pm Apr-Oct; ♿

The final stop on the Rubens trail (for Rubens himself) is his resting place, this Brabantine-Gothic church built between 1491 and 1656. Rubens painted *Our Lady Surrounded by Saints* specifically for his tomb – look closely and you'll see it's actually a family

---

NEW KID ON THE DOCKS

Currently under construction, the centrepiece of the revamped 19th-century docklands, 't Eilandje (little island; www.eilandje.be, in Dutch) is the purpose-built **Museum aan de Stroom** (MAS; ☎ 03 206 09 40; Hanze Stedenplaats) just north of the city centre. Designed like a spiral tower and topped with a city-viewing platform, MAS is set to become the city's defining history museum. Also under construction are stylised new dockside apartments, which in turn are attracting new drinking, dining and entertainment venues. Check with the tourist office for updates.

ACROSS THE RIVER

For the best view of the city skyline, take the vintage timber escalator or Art Deco elevator into the 1930s St-Anna pedestrian tunnel and follow it beneath the Scheldt river for 572m to reach the left (west) bank. The grassy parkland on this little-developed side of the river makes a scenic picnic spot. Heading around 1km north of the tunnel on the left bank brings you to St-Anna Strand, Antwerp's beach. Swimming in the murky river wouldn't be advised, even if it was tempting (it's not), but the beach still gets packed during the city's summertime festivities (p136).

portrait, starring Rubens as St George and his wives and father.

🜲 ST-PAULUSKERK

☎ 03 232 32 67; Veemarkt 13; admission free; ⏲ 2-5pm Mon-Sat; ♿

Although consecrated in 1571, the ornate Baroque tower of this former Dominican cloister wasn't added until 1679. As with all of Antwerp's finest churches, though, the real appeal is inside, where you'll find over 50 paintings (with works by Rubens and Van Dyck among them) and 200 elaborate sculptures.

🛍 SHOP

Antwerp lives up to its hype as a shopper's paradise, especially for fashion. The city's main pedestrianised drag, the Meir (and its eastern extension, Leysstraat), is lined with high street chain stores (Zara et al), while the fashion district (p128) also has some great retro homewares and *brocante* (bric-a-brac) on Kloosterstraat one block in from the river. For intimate art

galleries, bookshops, secondhand CDs and specialist music stores, head to Lange Koepoortstraat and Wolstraat, both northwest of St-Carolus Borromeuskerk. A wealth of shops are listed on the website www.antwerpshoppingstreets.be.

🛍 ANN DEMEULEMEESTER
Fashion

☎ 03 216 01 33; Verlatstraat 38; ⏲ 11am-7pm Mon-Sat

The monochrome men's and women's fashions of this Antwerp Six pioneer reflect the monastic backdrop of her flagship store in 't Zuid.

🛍 BURIE *Chocolate*

☎ 03 232 36 88; www.chobel.be; Korte Gasthuisstraat 3; ⏲ 9.30am-6pm Mon-Sat

Fronted by fantastical window displays, this historic chocolatier creates chocolates in all shapes and sizes, including 'Antwerp hands' (see Hands in the Air, p131) and brilliant-cut diamonds.

🏠 COCCODRILLO Shoes
☎ 03 233 20 93; Schuttershofstraat 9a;
🕐 11am-6pm Mon-Sat

Down-to-earth but by no means down-at-heel, this shoe boutique is a local institution, and is usually packed on Saturdays. This is the place to pick up big-name international brands as well as local designers.

🏠 COPYRIGHT Books
☎ 03 232 94 16; Nationalestraat 28a;
🕐 11am-6.30pm Tue-Sat, 11am-5.30pm Sun

Adjacent to the fashion museum, MoMu (p123), this specialist bookshop stocks fashion, art and architecture tomes in a minimalist whitewashed space.

🏠 DEL REY Chocolate
☎ 03 470 28 61; Appelmansstraat 5-9;
🕐 9am-6.30pm Mon-Sat, degustation salon 10am-6pm Mon-Sat

If the sweet vapours of chocolates being made out the back of this beautiful shop prove irresistible, you can get a taste on the spot at the adjoining degustation salon.

🏠 DE VAGANT SLIJTERIJ Jenever
☎ 03 233 15 38; Reyndersstraat;
🕐 11am-6pm Mon & Wed-Sat

After settling on your favourite flavour of jenever in the bar of the same name (p135), head across the street to this slijterij (liquor shop) stocking more than 200 varieties. Its line-up of bottles of all shapes, colours and sizes resemble an old-fashioned pharmacy, reflecting jenever's original medicinal purpose.

🏠 FISH & CHIPS Fashion
☎ 03 227 08 24; www.fishandchips.be;
Kammenstraat 36-38; 🕐 10am-6.30pm Mon-Sat

AREA OF INTEREST – FASHION QUARTER
Wedged between 't Zuid to the south and the historic district to the north, Antwerp's fashion quarter, St-Andries, continues to breed new and innovative designers and is prime territory for browsing, particularly along the following streets (highlighted on the map):
> Nationalestraat & side streets – for cutting-edge Antwerp/Belgian talent
> Kammenstraat – for young independent designers, retro and secondhand clothes, streetwear, skate/snowboard gear, piercings and tattoos
> Huidevettersstraat, Komedieplaats & Schuttershofstraat – for luxury labels like Cartier, Gucci and Louis Vuitton
The tourist office (p197) sells a 'fashion map' (€1.50), and for serious followers, a 'fashion walk' book (€10), with in-depth background on each designer.

Bart Willems
Fashion Designer

How did you get started? When I was 16 I was a handyman and put up shelves for Dries Van Noten and Dirk Bikkembergs (see p18). I was impressed with what they were doing – so dynamic. I then studied at the academy. **Who do you design for?** Men and children. **Design philosophy?** Wearable, comfortable, fun. **Hardest aspect of your work?** Looking into the future. At the end my designs have to sell. Not everyone is avant-garde; people like to feel they belong. **Annual work cycle?** First the trade fairs, to get a taste of everything and see the season's colours. Then competition shopping, identifying key shapes/lengths; developing 'stories'; sourcing manufacturers; and checking samples. **Will Belgium ever split?** Oh no. That would be a tragedy. Diversity's a big thing for Belgium. It's time to start a new era, *with* Belgium.

Lifelike stoner and skater mannequins are hard to tell apart from much of the clientele at this edgy streetwear emporium where DJs spin hard beats. The upstairs café is great for leafing through clubbing fliers over a freshly squeezed juice.

🏠 HET MODEPALEIS *Fashion*
☎ 03 470 25 10; www.driesvannoten.be; Nationalestraat 16; 🕙 10am-6.30pm Mon-Sat
Capped by a dome, this landmark 1881 curved, corner building is the elegant 'fashion palace' of Antwerp Six designer, Dries Van Noten, and worth a look for the architecture alone.

🏠 HUIS A BOON *Fashion*
☎ 03 232 33 87; Lombardenvest 2-4; 🕙 10am-6pm Mon-Sat
Staff at this 1884-established shop still slide forest-green leather boxes out from the oak shelves lining the walls, lifting the lid and unwrapping the tissue paper to show you the soft leather, kid and other delicate gloves nestled inside.

🏠 MEKANIK STRIP *Comics*
☎ 03 234 23 47; St-Jacobsmarkt 73; 🕙 10am-6pm Mon-Sat
This superb comic shop has a little art gallery upstairs, and has initiated Antwerp's own Comic Mural Route – see p16.

ANTWERP MARKETS
The city's oldest antique flea-market, **Vrijdagmarkt** (🕙 6-11am Fri), on the square of the same name, has been operating since the 16th century. Many a Sunday in Antwerp is spent trawling through the *brocante* **Rommelmarkt** (bric-a-brac market; St-Jansvliet; 🕙 7am-3pm Sun) near the river. For picnic fare, head to the city's main food market, **Vogelmarkt** (Theaterplein; 🕙 6am-3pm Sat & Sun).

🏠 STADSFEESTZAAL
Shopping Mall
Meir 78; 🕙 10am-7pm Mon-Sat
The 19th-century neoclassical architecture of this former city festival hall is jaw-dropping, particularly when viewed from the champagne-glass-shaped platform rising beneath its glass roof. The historic building was gutted by fire in 2001, and reopened in late 2007 as an ultra-upmarket shopping mall extending from the Meir south to Hopland, but the luxe boutiques are a bonus – the restored building is the real star.

🏠 VÉRONIQUE BRANQUINHO
Fashion
☎ 03 233 66 16; www.veronique branquinho.com; Nationalestraat 73; 🕙 11am-6pm Mon-Sat
Véronique Branquinho's classic tailoring for men and women has

confirmed her reputation as one of the new generations of fashion academy graduates to pick up the baton and run with it. Black features heavily in her collections, with occasional splashes of silver and gold.

🏠 WALTER *Fashion*
☎ 03 213 26 44; www.waltervanbeir endonck.com; St Antoniusstraat 12; 🕒 1-6pm Mon, 11am-6.30pm Tue-Sat
Antwerp Sixer Van Beirendonck now heads-up the fashion department at his alma mater around the corner, while displaying his outrageous menswear collections in this stark, gallery-like converted garage.

🍴 EAT
Fries are no less ubiquitous in Antwerp than elsewhere in Belgium, and the standards no less exacting. In the historic centre, try **Frituur No 1** (Hoogstraat 1).

🍴 BERLIN *Bistro* €€
☎ 03 227 11 01; Kleine Markt 1-3; 🕒 7.30am-1am Mon-Wed, 10am-3am Fri-Sun
A magnet for everyone from stylish shoppers to students using the free wi-fi, the black-painted Berlin is great for breakfast, homemade bistro fare or just a cocktail or beer.

🍴 DA VINCI *Italian* €€
☎ 03 237 41 71; Verschansingstraat 1
Most diners come to this casual-chic restaurant for its crispy, thin-crusted, woodfired pizzas but the kitchen also turns out classical pastas such as scallops in a creamy piquant sauce.

🍴 DANSING CHOCOLA *Bistro* €
☎ 03 237 19 05; Kloosterstraat 159; 🕒 10am-1am Sun-Thu, 10am-2am Fri & Sat
Things get loose at this old-fashioned café, with staff grooving behind the bar or vaulting Tarzan-like up to the wrought-iron

---

HANDS IN THE AIR
Legend has it that the city's name comes from the Dutch *hand werpen* (hand throwing). The story goes that a giant named Druon Antigoon forced shipmasters to pay a toll to pass through on the Scheldt river, until Roman warrior Silvius Brabo hacked off Antigoon's hand and hurled it in the water.

OK, so the more likely origin of the name is the alluvial mound *(aanwerp)* on which the Steen (p125) was built, but you'll find everything from biscuits to chocolates in the shape of *Antwerpse handjes* (Antwerp hands), and, on the Grote Markt, a fountain featuring a statue of Brabo holding the giant's hand aloft.

mezzanine railing to take orders, while busking violinists serenade diners. Dishes – Belgian and a few international options like spicy Thai soup – are simple and incredibly filling (go for 'small' portions unless you're ravenous), and there are sensational fries (€3 a bowlful). The kitchen closes at 10pm.

🍴 DE KLEINE ZAVEL
Seafood   €€€
☎ 03 231 96 91; Stoofstraat 2;
🕑 noon-2pm Sun-Fri & 6-10pm Sun-Thu, 6.30-10.30pm Fri & Sat
Flavours of the Med mix with freshly caught fish (and a handful of meat dishes), accompanied by an outstanding wine list, at this celebrated yet resolutely humble restaurant.

🍴 GIN FISH *Seafood*   €€€
☎ 03 231 32 07; Haarstraat; 🕑 6.30-10pm Tue-Sat
In the absence of printed menus, diners congregate around the bar facing the open kitchen to watch chef Didier Garnich create gastronomical feasts from the day's freshest market ingredients. Garnich famously relinquished his formerly Michelin-starred establishment De Matelote, and Gin Fish now has its own newly minted star. You'll need to book at least two weeks ahead on the weekend, but if you're lucky you

might be able to snag a midweek seat the same morning.

🍴 GRAND CAFÉ HORTA
Brasserie   €€
☎ 03 232 28 15; Hopland 2; 🕑 9am-9pm Tue-Sun
Encased in glass with views from the basement bar up to street level, this café-restaurant has outsized iron girders – relics salvaged from Victor Horta's much-mourned Art Nouveau masterpiece, Maison du Peuple (see p160). Stop for a drink, snack or a full meal, with Mediterranean-inspired choices like asparagus risotto or ravioli with polenta, or that brasserie classic: steak-and-chips.

🍴 HOFFY'S *Jewish*   €€
☎ 03 234 35 35; Lange Kievitstraat 52; 🕑 11am-10pm Sun-Thu, 11am-6pm Fri, closed Sat
Past the deli counter displaying platters of salads, sliced meats and baked goods are a succession of tiled dining rooms with Deco-style uplights and rose-coloured wallpaper, where you can enjoy well-priced lunches (around €15), or quality Chateaubriand or rib-eye steaks for dinner.

🍴 HUNGRY HENRIETTA
Belgian   €€
☎ 03 232 29 28; Lombardenvest 19; 🕑 noon-2pm & 6-9pm Mon-Fri

Fashion buyers cut deals over seafood bisque, crispy-skinned ray with capers, and seared scallops on a bed of mashed potato in Henrietta's glossy black-lacquered and polished-concrete interior, or on the outdoor terrace. Call ahead as it's periodically closed during school holidays.

🍴 KLEINBLATT *Bakery* €
Map p122; ☎ 03 226 00 18; Provinciestraat 206; ⏰ 6am-6.30pm Sun-Thu, 6am-4pm Fri, closed Sat
A tantalising array of freshly baked breads and feather-light biscuits has kept loyal patrons lining up at this Jewish bakery/pâtisserie since 1903. One small biscuit is around €0.60, but the quality is supreme.

🍴 LOMBARDIA *Organic* €
☎ 03 233 68 19; Lombardenvest 78; ⏰ 8am-6pm Mon-Sat
Everything at this hip lunch bar is organic, from pies, sandwiches and a bounty of salads, right down to the milkshakes. In summer, come early to claim a shaded table on the terrace.

🍴 LUCY CHANG *Asian* €€
☎ 03 248 95 60; www.lucychang.be; Marnixplaats 16-17; ⏰ noon-midnight
Thanks to the variety of seating options (from bar stools to banquettes), solo diners, couples and groups of friends all feel at home at this Asian market–style restaurant serving well-priced, well-prepared cuisine from around the continent (Japanese fried noodles, Malaysian curry soup, Pad Thai and more). Is located near the southern end of Nationalestraat.

🍴 PASTA *Italian* €€
☎ 03 213 16 86; www.apm-hippo.be; Oude Koornmarkt 32; ⏰ 11am-late Mon-Sat, 6pm-late Sun
Soaring squid-ink-coloured walls and gleaming dark timber furniture create an ambient setting for classy pastas and meat and fish dishes. The bountiful portions give Pasta one of the best price to quality ratios in the historic centre.

🍴 POTTENBRUG *Bistro* €€
☎ 03 231 51 47; Minderbroedersrui 38; ⏰ noon-2pm & 6-10pm Mon-Fri, 6-10pm Sat
Vintage posters, cosy tables and a lovely alfresco terrace make this old bistro an enduring favourite for authentic and hearty local dishes.

🍴 SIR ANTHONY VAN DIJCK *Flemish* €€€
☎ 03 231 61 70; www.siranthonyvandijck.be; Oude Koornmarkt 16; ⏰ lunch & dinner Mon-Sat by reservation
Hidden in a tiny, cobbled laneway in a 16th-century building, this

Jenever know unless you try at *jenever* café De Vagant

exquisite restaurant is among Antwerp's finest for Flemish cuisine with flair; best appreciated over its four-course 'gourmet' menu (€45).

▼ DRINK

▼ BAR TABAC *Bar*
Waalsekaai 43; 🕑 **8pm-late Wed-Mon**
If this tiny Provençal bar is closed, you can be sure everywhere in Antwerp's shut down for the night. Corral a metal table inside or a salvaged cinema seat on the terrace. Has regular DJs and drinks specials.

▼ BIERHUIS KULMINATOR
Beer Pub
☎ **03 232 45 38; Vleminckveld 32;**
🕑 **8pm-late Mon, 11am-late Tue-Fri, 5pm-late Sat**
Beneath a vine-draped ceiling, this cluttered pub is a veritable library of Belgian beers, with over 750 varieties catalogued in a menu so long the categories (including some vintages from the 1970s) are colour-coded. On-tap specials are listed on the blackboard.

▼ CAFÉ BEVEREN *Pub*
☎ **03 231 22 25; www.cafebeveren.com, in Dutch; Vlasmarkt 2;** 🕑 **noon-late Mon & Thu-Sun**

This time-worn treasure is a favourite with sailors, students and retro fiends for its antique jukebox and organ.

☿ DE NIEUWE LINDE *Bar*
☎ 03 248 14 86; Pacificatiestraat 49;
☽ 5pm-late
Cheap beers and local artworks hung on the walls and painted on the ceiling make this a popular hangout for artists and writers. There's good background music, if you can hear it over the animated conversations.

☿ DE VAGANT *Jenever Café*
☎ 03 233 15 38; Reyndersstraat 21;
☽ noon-late
The tiled floors and old advertising posters on the wall evoke a classic neighbourhood café, but De Vagant's main draw is its staggering 200-plus varieties of *jenever*,

with a daily special chalked on the blackboard.

☿ ELFDE GEBOD *Pub*
☎ 03 289 34 66; Torfbrug 10;
☽ noon-late
The eyes of dozens of statues of saints and other religious figures watch you while you drink beers at the shrine-like 'Eleventh Commandment'.

☿ KING KONG BAR *Bar*
☎ 03 216 37 77; Volkstraat 58;
☽ 11.30am-midnight Tue-Thu, 11.30am-4am Fri-Sun, closed Mon
With art installation–like décor throughout its lounge-style rooms, the slick King Kong Bar epitomises Antwerp's sense of style. Finding the bathrooms takes you on a magical mystery tour up two flights of creaking wooden stairs.

☿ PAETERS VAETJE *Pub*
☎ 03 231 84 76; Blauwmoezelstraat 1; ☽ 11am-3am Sun-Thu, 11am-5am Fri & Sat
On a bleak, rain-swept afternoon, there's no cosier spot to hole up than this snug *bruin eetcafé* ('brown eating café', see p164), with glowing lamps illuminating its dark timber main room and upper-level mezzanine. Dishes are simple and inexpensive, and the beer selection excellent.

🍸 PELGROM *Pub*
☎ 03 234 08 09; www.pelgrom.be; Pelgrimsstraat 18; ⏰ 5pm-late Mon-Fri, noon-late Sat & Sun

From the street you'd never guess it was here. But heading past a flickering open fire and down a narrow flight of stairs brings you into this cavernous cross-vaulted medieval cellar spanning several rooms, with long candlelit tables. If you're lucky you may catch the house magician; Pelgrom also serves 'medieval'-style feasts (around €18 for a main).

🍸 POPI CAFÉ *Gay & Lesbian*
☎ 03 238 15 30; Plantinkaai 12; ⏰ 2pm-1am Mon-Thu, 2pm-late Fri-Sun

Popi Café's 'afternoon tea and crumpets' (accompanied by boppy music) hints at the tongue-in-cheek nature of this long-standing hangout. A good first stop for sussing out the scene.

🍸 'T WAAGSTUK *Beer Pub*
☎ 03 225 02 19; Stadswaag 20; ⏰ 10am-2am Sun-Thu, 2pm-4am Fri & Sat

Dozens of steins are suspended from the ceiling of this special-ist beer pub accessed through a gate inside a medieval courtyard. It's a favourite with students (and their professors) from the nearby university.

🍸 THEO *Café, Shoes*
☎ 03 226 79 19; Nationalestraat 33; ⏰ 9am-7pm Mon-Sat, noon-6pm Sun in summer, 9am-6pm Mon-Sat in winter

Not just a café and not just a chic footwear boutique, but both. You can sip a decent coffee and nibble on Parisian Poilâne bread while checking out the soft-leather shoes for sale.

⭐ PLAY

Antwerp has a sumptuous cultural calendar. Tickets for performances can be bought direct from the venues, or from FNAC (p169).

⭐ BUSTER *Live Music*
☎ 03 232 51 53; www.busterpodium.be; Kaasrui 1; ⏰ 8pm-late

Buster's mixed-bag programme includes Tuesday's live concerts (mainly jazz and rock; around €10) as well as its traditional Thursday

---

HOT IN THE CITY
Oh baby. Antwerp is a party hot spot, with bars, clubs and venues firing year-round. But the city is at its hottest during the **Zomer van Antwerpen** (summer of Antwerp; www.zomer vanantwerpen.be), which is essentially a non-stop party that runs throughout July and August. Many concerts and other events take place outdoors, in-cluding along the river – look out for posters around town.

jam sessions (free). Stand-up comedians and actors trying out material also do stage time here (in Dutch or English).

☆ CAFÉ D'ANVERS *Club*
☎ 03 226 38 70; www.café-d-anvers .com; Verversrui 15; admission €10; ⏲ 11pm-7.30am Fri & Sat
Belgian and international DJs spin funk, house, disco, soul and more at this tireless club in a refurbished church in the city's red-light district.

☆ CAFÉ HOPPER *Jazz, Blues*
☎ 03 248 49 33; www.hopperjazz.org, in Dutch; Leopold De Waelstraat 2

Live jazz and blues take place at this small, smart venue usually on Sunday, Monday and Wednesday (around €8 for established acts).

☆ CAFÉ LOCAL *Club*
☎ 03 238 50 04; www.cafelocal.be; Waalsekaai 25; ⏲ 10pm-late Tue-Sat
Styled like a crumbling Cuban backstreet, Café Local is a mecca for salsa and world music, as well as disco – check the agenda online and expect to pay between €5 to €10 admission.

☆ CARTOONS *Cinema*
☎ 03 232 96 32; www.cartoons-cinema .be, in Dutch; Kaasstraat 4-6

Never far from view, the beautiful Onze Lieve Vrouwekathedraal (p125) is still a crowd pleaser

RED, RED LIGHTS

Any major port has a red-light district, and Antwerp's stretches roughly between St-Paulusplaats and Verversrui. All up, though, it's pretty tame, and certainly pales (or perhaps blushes) in comparison to its counterpart in neighbouring Amsterdam, although the latter is in the process of being tamed, too.

Catch arthouse and quality foreign films on this alternative cinema's three screens before or after a drink, or snack at the cosy on-site café (open from 5.30pm Monday to Saturday, from 3.30pm Sunday). Tickets are discounted on Mondays.

⭐ DE MUZE *Jazz*
☎ 03 226 01 26; Melkmarkt 15;
🕐 noon-4am
This venerable café winds over three wooden storeys separated by curtains of fairy-lights. Musos (mainly local) take to the stage from 10pm Monday to Saturday and at 3pm on Sunday, during which time drinks cost an extra €0.50, with proceeds going to the performers. Gig schedules are posted on the door.

⭐ DE ROMA *Cinema*
☎ 03 235 04 90; www.deroma.be, in Dutch; Turnhoutsebaan 286
Residents of the neighbourhood of Borgerhout, east of Centraal

Station, volunteered their time, money and love of cinema to restore this 1928 building to its original splendour. Tram 10 and 24 stop out front.

⭐ DESINGEL *Concert Hall*
☎ 03 248 28 28; www.desingel.be; Desguinlei 25
This striking, concrete box houses two concert halls, which between them form Antwerp's main venue for classical music, international theatre and modern dance. From Centraal Station or Groenplaats, take tram 2 in the direction of Hoboken to the deSingel stop.

⭐ KONINGIN ELISABETHZAAL *Concert Hall*
☎ 0900 260 00; www.fccc.be, in Dutch; Koningin Astridplein 23-24
Flanders' philharmonic orchestra, **De Filharmonie** (www.defilharmonie.be), among others, plays at this concert hall located next to Centraal Station.

⭐ KONINKLIJK BALLET VAN VLAANDEREN *Ballet*
☎ 03 234 34 38; www.koninklijk balletvanvlaanderen.be; Westkaai 16
Belgium's only ballet company occupies a purpose-built building in 't Eilandje, at the northern edge of the city centre. Performances take place here and at the Vlaamse Opera (p140).

Bask in the glow of all that jazz at De Muze

⭐ PETROL *Club*
☎ 03 226 49 63; www.petrolclub.be, in Dutch; 21 d'Herbouvillekaai; admission varies

Reggae, electronica, drum and bass and more make this pumpin' venue a perennial favourite, as does the relaxed dress code, which keeps things (pretty much) pretension-free. It's about a 2km walk (or taxi ride) from 't Zuid.

⭐ RED & BLUE *Gay & Lesbian*
☎ 03 213 05 55; www.redandblue .be; Lange Schipperskapelstraat 11-13; admission €7.50 plus €2 membership fee; ⏰ 11pm-7am Sat plus special events

Saturdays attract hot-blooded gay guys from far and wide, while regular Café de Love parties are for lesbians 'and their male soul mates'. The website also links to the club's mixed-crowd fixtures, such as Studio 54, and We Love Thursdays.

⭐ STEREO SUSHI
Club, Restaurant
☎ 03 248 67 27; www.stereosushi.be; Luikstraat 6; ⏰ bar & restaurant 6pm-late Wed-Sun, club Thu-Sat until 5am

Hipsters head to this anime-adorned, fuchsia-tinged place for platters of sushi before grooving to DJs like the Milkshakerz and the Breakbeatles. Just how strict the door policy is depends on how busy things are, but glamming up is *de rigueur* here in any case.

⭐ VLAAMSE OPERA *Opera*
☎ 03 233 66 85; www.vlaamseopera.be; Frankrijklei 3

Built in 1907, this marble-lined opera house is a dramatic setting for performances by the resident Koninklijke Vlaamse Opera (Royal Flemish Opera). Tickets range between €9 and €95.

Good company and fine surrounds along Graslei

>GHENT

Smack in the middle of Brussels, Bruges and Antwerp, Ghent (Gent in Dutch, Gand in French) is the most unheralded of this quartet. Yet it distils their greatest attributes into one engaging and enchanting city.

Ghent's confluence of rivers crisscrossed by Parisian-style bridges, its turreted castle and cobbled streets lined with step-gabled buildings rival Bruges' beauty. Its longstanding artistic traditions have spurred creative industries and galleries that are as cutting-edge as Antwerp's. And it shares Brussels' diversity and energy. Over one quarter of Ghent's 235,000-strong population is made up of university students, infusing the city with alternative live music, packed pubs, cheap eateries, and lively open-air markets and oyster bars.

The city's graceful historic centre is almost completely car-free (Europe's largest such zoning), substituting blaring horns and exhaust fumes for a vibrant street life that peaks during July's 10-day Gentse Feesten (p29) the biggest street festival on the continent.

GHENT

◉ SEE

◉ SHOP

◉ EAT

◉ DRINK

◉ PLAY

GHENT

 SEE

The most serene way to see the city is by watching it float past from aboard a boat – see p196 for cruise information.

BELFORT

☎ 09 233 39 54; St-Baafsplein; adult/concession/under 12 yr €3/2.50/free; ⏰ 10am-6pm mid-Mar to mid-Nov

Stupendous views over Ghent unfurl from the top of this Unesco-listed belfry built in the 14th century. Its enormous Kloke Roeland bell was used to warn the town of enemy invasion and some 54 bells ring out across the city from its carillon. You can scale the steps or take the small elevator (though it doesn't accommodate wheelchairs).

DR GUISLAIN MUSEUM

☎ 09 216 35 95; www.museumdrguislain.be; Jozef Guislainstraat 43; adult/concession/under 12 yr €5/2.50/free; ⏰ 9am-5pm Tue-Fri, 1-5pm Sat & Sun; ♿

Anyone unnerved by *One Flew Over the Cuckoos' Nest* should avoid it – this former psychiatric hospital, northwest of the city centre, showcases some chilling forms of treatment, and also features a collection of art by 'outsiders'.

GRAVENSTEEN

☎ 09 225 93 06; St Veerleplein; adult/concession/under 12 yr €6/1.20/free; ⏰ 9am-6pm Apr-Sep, 9am-5pm Oct-Mar

The counts of Flanders wielded their power from Ghent's 12th-century castle in the centre of town. Rising up out of the water, its square cut towers and ramparts are the stuff of storybooks. To get a feel for its slings-and-arrows history, rent the evocative multimedia guide (€3).

MUSEUM VOOR SCHONE KUNSTEN

☎ 09 240 07 00; www.mskgent.be; Citadelpark; adult/concession/under 12 yr & 10am-1pm Sun €4/2.50/free; ⏰ 10am-6pm Tue-Sun

Fresh from an extensive renovation, the Museum of Fine Arts contains a varied collection of early and modern art including some

ART EXPLAINED

Free guided tours of Ghent's **Museum voor Schone Kunsten** (Museum of Fine Arts; above), **Museum voor Vormgeving** (Design Museum; opposite) and **Stedelijk Museum voor Actuele Kunst** (SMAK; Museum of Contemporary Art; p146) take place at 11am on Sundays at each of the museums by reservation (call the museums or contact the tourist office (p197) during which time entry is also free.

SURVIVAL OF A MASTERPIECE

It's somewhat miraculous that *The Adoration of the Mystic Lamb* (below) is still here. The Calvinists nearly destroyed it and Austria's prudish Emperor Joseph II had Adam and Eve replaced with clothed versions (the original nudes are now back in place, and the replacements are also on show). During the French Revolution it was marched off to Paris, and it was snatched during WWII by the Germans who hid it in an Austrian salt mine, where it was nearly blown up. The *De Rechtvaardige Rechters* (The Fair Judges) panel, stolen in 1934, has never been found, a copy occupies its place.

Flemish Primitives and a couple of typically nightmarish works by Hieronymus Bosch including *De Kruisdraging* (Bearing of the Cross; c1480), depicting hideous characters mocking Christ.

🄲 MUSEUM VOOR VORMGEVING

☎ 09 267 99 99; http://design.museum .gent.be/; Jan Breydelstraat 5; adult/ concession/under 12 yr & 10am-1pm Sun €2.50/1.20/free; ☯ 10am-6pm Tue-Sun
Behind its 18th-century façade, Ghent's Design Museum displays furnishings from the Renaissance to today in a striking modern space. Art Deco, Art Nouveau and retro (including some lurid '70s sofas) are all represented, and there are regular temporary exhibits (sometimes attracting an additional fee).

🄲 ST-BAAFSKATHEDRAAL & THE ADORATION OF THE MYSTIC LAMB

☎ 09 269 20 45; St-Baafsplein; admission free for cathedral, The Adoration

of the Mystic Lamb adult/under 12 yr €3/free; ☯ cathedral 8.30am-6pm Apr-Oct, to 5pm Nov-Mar, The Adoration of the Mystic Lamb 9.30am-5pm Mon-Sat & 1-5pm Sun Apr-Oct, 10.30am-4pm Mon-Sat & 1-4pm Sun Nov-Mar; ♿
Flemish Primitive artist Jan Van Eyck's richly detailed 20-panel altarpiece, *De Aanbidding van het Lam*

Spoilt for choice – St-Baafskathedraal and Belfort

It's a bush, right? Perspective is everything at Stedelijk Museum voor Actuele Kunst (SMAK)

Gods (The Adoration of the Mystic Lamb; 1432) is one of the earliest-known oil paintings in existence and the highlight of Ghent's 22-altar, stained-glass-adorned cathedral. A rare depiction of God the Father can be seen on the altarpiece's upper tier, while the lower tier features the eponymous lamb, symbolising Christ's sacrifice. The altarpiece's survival defies the odds – see p145.

STEDELIJK MUSEUM VOOR ACTUELE KUNST (SMAK)
☎ 09 240 76 01; www.smak.be; Citadelpark; adult/concession/under 12 yr & 10am-1pm Sun €6/4/free; 10am-6pm Tue-Sun; ♿

Many people visit Ghent for its Museum of Contemporary Art. It holds a highly regarded permanent collection of local works (including Karel Appel, Pierre Alechinsky and Panamarenko) and works of international celebrities (like Christo, Warhol and Hockney), though it's been packing these away to devote its space to single major exhibits (such as Paul McCarthy's blood-spattered installations), so it's worth checking the programme.

🛍 SHOP
Since Ghent's city centre became car-free over a decade ago, shops selling heavy items (such as

GRAFFITI STREET
To keep Ghent's ancient architecture graffiti-free, the city has allocated one street, the pedestrian lane of Werregarenstraat, for legal tagging. The high walls running the 100m of this narrow passageway form an ideal canvas for graffiti artists to make their mark and many well-known artists come to Ghent to tag here. Feel free to spray away too.

furniture) have moved out to areas accessible for drivers. Veldstraat is where you'll find department and high street chain stores; things get more interesting around Mageleinstraat, to the east, with boutiques and specialist shops. Some of the city's quirkier shops cluster on and around Serpenstraat.

🏠 **CARGO** *Lighting*
☎ 09 224 13 41; www.cargo-art.be; Krommewal 1; ⏰ 10am-12.30pm & 2-6pm Tue-Sat
Artistic lighting designs at this showroom/workshop incorporate natural elements such as oversize cones and back-lit square wall-mountings made from diverse materials ranging from mussel shells to recycled industrial materials.

🏠 **EVA BOS** *Fashion*
☎ 0495 49 61 64; Vlaanderenstraat 66; ⏰ 10.30am-12.30pm & 1.30-6pm Tue-Fri, 11am-6pm Sat

Eva Bos, fashion designer and teacher at Ghent's fashion academy, sources 'the real treasures' from the '50s and '60s to stock at her vintage boutique. There are also new designs here, including some by Eva's most talented students.

🏠 **SJAPOO** *Fashion*
☎ 09 225 75 35; Sluizeken 29; ⏰ 10am-1pm & 2-6pm Tue-Fri, 11am-6.30pm Sat
Milliner Ria Dewilde's atelier is out the back of her boutique (north of Vrijdagmarkt), where she sells her one-off creations. Many are crafted along 1920s lines for everyday wear, as well as more elaborate hats for weddings and christenings. Ria also sells hand-picked Belgian- and French-design clothing.

🏠 **TEMMERMAN** *Confectionary*
☎ 09 224 00 41; Kraanlei 79; ⏰ 11am-6pm Wed-Sat
Glass jars filled with sweets line up behind the counter of this old-fashioned sweet shop, which has been in its current location since 1904, and is run by the eighth generation of this family of confectioners. All of its sweets are made by the family's factory, including typically Belgian *neuzekes* (hard, triangular cherry-red 'noses' filled with soft jelly) and *mokke* (aniseed biscuits).

GHENT

HANGING AROUND

So why is a noose hanging in a charming old sweet shop like **Temmerman** (p147)? It's not a Hansel-and-Gretel-style punishment, but an ancient Ghent tradition. In 1537 Emperor Charles V sentenced Ghent's uprising citizens to the public humiliation of walking the streets barefoot wearing just a shirt, and a noose around their neck. This walk is re-enacted during festivities, with the *stropdragers* (noose wearers) honouring their ancestors' rebellion (ask the tourist office for dates). Look out for nooses in other unlikely spots around town.

🖂 TIERENTEYN-VERLENT
Artisan Products

☎ 09 225 83 36; www.tierenteyn-verlent
.be; Groentenmarkt 3; ⏰ 8.30am-6pm
Mon-Fri, 8.30am-12.30pm & 1-6pm Sat

Ghent's traditional mustard-maker, the 1790-established Tierenteyn-Verlent, has occupied this heritage-listed shop since 1860, and it retains its original interior of tall glass cabinets of apothecary and spice jars behind varnished timber counters. Mustard is still made using original techniques and only natural ingredients: vinegar, salt and ground mustard seeds. Each jar comes with its own little wooden spoon (plastic spoons can also be used, but not metal, as it separates the vinegar).

🍴 EAT

There's ongoing debate about who makes Ghent's best fries, but you can't go wrong at **Frituur Filip** (Pensmarkt; ⏰ 11.30am-1.30pm & 5-10.30pm Mon-Thu, 11.30am-midnight Fri-Sun), who's been here as long as anyone can remember.

🍴 DE 3 BIGGETJES
Gastronomic   €€€

☎ 09 224 46 48; www.de3biggetjes
.com, in Dutch; Zeugsteeg 7; ⏰ noon-2pm & 7-9.30pm Mon-Tue & Thu-Fri, 7-9.30pm Sat

Situated on 'sow street' in the tangle of lanes making up Patershol (p150) 'the three piglets' is a gastronomic gem, with incredible fusion dishes and good-value fixed-price menus (€16 for lunch, and €29 for a three-course dinner, or €39 for a four-course evening meal including champagne) in an intimate setting.

🍴 DE GEKROONDE HOOFDEN
Belgian   €€

☎ 09 233 37 74; www.degekroon
dehoofden.be, in Dutch; Burgstraat 4; ⏰ 6pm-midnight Mon-Sat, 6-11pm Sun

Spare ribs (in honey, natural, and the house version, sweet and sour) are the speciality of this large, airy restaurant situated footsteps from Ghent's castle. You can fill up on them à la carte (from €15) or as part of all-you-can-eat deals (€23 to €37), finished off with chocolate mousse. Staff are welcoming and genuine.

☷ ETABLESSEMENT MAX
Brasserie €

☎ 09 223 97 31; Goudenleeuwplein 3; ⏱ 9am-6pm Mon, Wed & Thu, 9am-late Fri-Sun, closed Tue

This elegant, pale-pistachio-and-gold brasserie serving refined fare is run by Yves Van Maldeghem (p151) whose entrepreneurial family started out with a grand mobile fair stall. Yves bakes waffles using his family's 120-year-old waffle irons, and also makes pancakes and sizzling apple

---

GHENT MARKETS
The city's car-free streets and open-air squares, such as those listed below, are tailor-made for markets.
Ajuinlei (⏱ 8am-1pm Sun) Book market along the river quays.
Groentenmarkt (⏱ 9am-1pm Fri) Organic market and an oyster bar.
Kouter (⏱ 8am-1pm Sun) Flowers, food and an oyster bar.
St-Jacobs (⏱ 8am-1pm Fri-Sun) Flea market.
St-Michielsplein (⏱ 7.30am-1pm Sun) Food market.
Vrijdagmarkt Food market (⏱ 7.30am-1pm Fri); Bird market (⏱ 7.30am-1pm Sun).

---

fritters. To bake your own, pick up Jan Gheysens' *Belgian Waffles and Other Treats* (2006) here, which contains Yves' family recipes.

☷ HET GROOT VLEESHUIS
Flemish €

☎ 09 223 23 24; www.grootvleeshuis .be; Groentenmarkt 7; ⏱ restaurant 11.30am-3pm Tue-Fri, 11.30am-4pm Sat & Sun, shop & bar 10am-6pm Tue-Sun

Only products from the surrounding province are sold at this medieval butchers' hall, which has been converted into a shop selling artisan products (with free counter tastings of cheeses and meats). That means you won't find Coke on the menu in the attached glassed-in restaurant overlooking the old covered market's ceilings strung with hams, but you will find local brews, apple wine and, naturally, meat galore.

☷ HOUSE OF ELIOTT *Bistro* €€€

☎ 09 225 21 28; www.thehouseofeliott .be, in Dutch & French; Jan Breydelstraat 36; ⏱ noon-2pm & 6pm-late Thu-Mon

Flamboyantly camp turn-of-the-20th-century décor here includes period-dressed mannequins and candelabras in the street-level parlour/dining room, and old coffee grinders, sewing machines and Wedgwood-tiled walls in the basement 'servants' quarters'. The latter opens to a terrace jutting right over the canal, and features a tank full of live lobsters, the house speciality.

🍴 MARCO POLO *Italian* €€

☎ 09 225 04 20; Serpenstraat 11; ⏱ noon-2.30pm & 6-10pm Tue-Fri, 6-10pm Sat & Sun

This rustic slow-food restaurant looks like it's been lifted out of Piedmont's vine-ribboned hills. Peer from the communal wooden tables in the beamed dining room to the open kitchen to watch the chefs prepare market-fresh Italian classics (chalked daily on the blackboard menu).

🍴 MOSQUITO COAST
International €

☎ 09 224 37 20; www.mosquitocoast.be; Hoogpoort 28; ⏱ kitchen noon-2pm & 6-11pm Tue-Sat, bar 11am-late Tue-Sat

Dine on world dishes – from tapas to kangaroo steaks to stir-fries – in mosaic-tiled velour booths on the mezzanine, or in the bamboo-shaded courtyard or roof terrace at this large, airy 'travel and adventure café'. Stop by any time for a house mojito and a browse through the guidebooks in the bar filled with licence plates, road signs, currencies, maps and globes.

🍴 PAKHUIS *Brasserie* €€

☎ 09 223 55 55; www.pakhuis.be; Schuurkenstraat 4; ⏱ kitchen noon-11pm Sun-Thu, noon-midnight Fri & Sat, bar 11.30am-1am Sun-Thu, 11.30am-2am Fri & Sat

Soaring iron girders, interior balconies and a vaulted glass ceiling make this former warehouse a sublime setting for a Bloody Mary and/or a meal. Pakhuis excels in seafood (such as sea bass with puréed artichokes and vermouth sauce, or grilled Scottish salmon); wide-ranging seasonal choices might include lamb stew in Barbera wine, or organic pasta with black truffles.

AREA OF INTEREST – PATERSHOL

This ancient quarter of Ghent's inner city is built around a 14th-century former Carmelite monastery, which today often mounts free art exhibitions (ask the tourist office for programmes). Look for the low blue-painted wooden door on the corner of Trommelstraat and Plotersgracht. This 'hole', from which the area takes its name (Patershol translates as 'Monk's hole'), gave the monks direct access to the watercourse below, serving as a kind of early fire hydrant. Regenerated a few decades ago, Patershol's warren of cobbled laneways is now dotted with atmospheric, upmarket restaurants such as De 3 Biggetjes (p148).

Ψ| Yves Van Maldeghem
Waffle Baker/Brasserie Owner

When did you start baking waffles? My family invented the Brussels waffle here in 1839; I'm the sixth generation. It's in my blood. My grandmother taught me when I was nine years old, and I sold my first waffle that year at a fair. **Why is it called the Brussels waffle when it was invented in Ghent?** As the capital, Brussels was seen as more bourgeois, so people preferred to eat 'Brussels waffles'. **What's the secret of a perfect Brussels waffle?** It has to be crispy on the outside and the colour of wood – the colour of a Flemish oak tree. The main issue is making the inside fresh but not too moist. Gas is essential to control the temperature; I would rather close my business than use electricity. **Will Belgium ever split?** I don't know but it doesn't interest me – I'm only interested in baking waffles. (See also p51).

SOUPLOUNGE *Soup* €
☎ 09 223 62 03; www.souplounge.be, in Dutch; Zuivelbrugstraat 6; ⏲ 10am-7pm
The premise at this brightly lit eatery with perspex furnishings is simple and satisfying: a choice of four soups each day accompanied by bread and butter and fresh fruit. It also has filled baguettes and salads.

🍸 DRINK
See also listings under Eat and Play for more options.

CAFÉ DEN TURK *Pub*
☎ 09 233 01 97; www.cafedenturk.be; Botermarkt 3; ⏲ 11am-late
This venerable place dates *way* back to 1228, making it easily Ghent's oldest pub. But despite its 680-plus years, it remains true to its roots as a local gathering spot, and is the kind of place where you go in alone and come out knowing a dozen people.

CASA ROSA *Gay & Lesbian*
☎ 09 269 28 16; www.casarosa.be; Belfortstraat 39; ⏲ 3pm-1am
The 'Pink House' is an essential stop for gay and lesbian travellers to Ghent. The foyer bar attracts a mixed crowd, who can steer you to the latest hot spots. You'll also find a gay and lesbian information office (generally open business

hours on Monday, Wednesday and Saturday), and stands with city maps listing nightlife options and various other gay- and lesbian-friendly establishments.

DE HEL *Bar*
☎ 09 224 32 40; Kraanlei 81; ⏲ 4pm-late Tue-Sat, 2pm-late Sun
In an ornate baroque house, De Hel's black velveteen curtains, snug banquettes and candles flickering in red glass create a romantic ambience, and a complete change from bigger, brasher student bars.

HET WATERHUIS AAN DE BIERKANT *Beer Pub*
☎ 09 225 06 80; www.waterhuisaan derbierkant.be; Groentenmarkt 9; ⏲ 11am-late
Staff with a passion for beer serve over 140 brews in Waterhuis' cosy interior and on its sprawling riverside terrace. Exclusive house brews include a knockout amber Klokke Roeland (11% alcohol and often drunk as a nightcap; with a limit of three per person) and a blonde Gandavum Dry Hopping (7.5% and quite possibly the best beer this author's ever tasted). Unmissable.

MOKABON *Coffee Bar*
☎ 09 225 71 95; Donkersteeg 35; ⏲ 8am-7pm Mon-Sat year-round & 11.30am-6.30pm Sun Oct-Easter

The pungent aroma of coffee pervades your senses at this unpretentious coffee bar, which roasts its beans on the premises. Locals from all walks of life gather around the original Art Deco timber bar for hot coffee as well as iced coffee frappés. You can also buy the house-blend beans (ground or unground) for €13.20 per kilo.

SIMON SAYS Coffee Bar €
☎ 09 233 03 43; www.simon-says.be; Sluizeken 8; ⏱ 9am-6pm Tue-Fri, 10am-6pm Sat & Sun, later in summer
Inside one of Ghent's only Art Nouveau buildings, this creative little newcomer has gold futuristic flying objects hand-drawn on its turquoise walls by celebrated contemporary Antwerp artist, Panamarenko. Great for light organic lunches and snacks and Fairtrade coffee. Simon also runs a state-of-the-art two-room B&B upstairs. Located just north of Vrijdagmarkt.

'T DREUPELKOT Jenever Café
☎ 09 224 21 20; Groentenmarkt 12; ⏱ 11am-1am Tue-Sun
This convivial waterfront café adjacent to Het Waterhuis serves countless varieties of jenever.

'T VELOOTJE Bar
Kalversteeg 2
Push through the heavy, unmarked door and take care not to trip over old bikes, or whack your head on the kero lamps cluttering this tiny, darkened garage as you take a seat at a low wooden picnic table. Lieven De Vos has turned his bicycle workshop into an informal bar, of sorts – ask for a beer and Lieven will bring out whatever he selects; his opening hours are 'whenever I feel like opening until it closes down' (try after 9pm).

HOW TO ORDER BEER ACROSS A CROWDED BELGIAN BAR
You're in a seething pub, wondering how the bartender will hear you over the top of the din, when you see locals flashing a series of hand signals then, voila, receive their beers. Actually, ordering is easy. First, indicate how many beers you want by raising the corresponding number of fingers. Then indicate the type of beer you'd like with the following signals:
> Pintje – Raise your little finger. Gets you a standard glass of the house tap beer (such as Jupiler), usually 25cL, but sometimes 33cL, depending on the pub and the beer.
> Palmke – Clap against your lower palm. Gets you a glass of amber beer brewed by Palm.
> Duvel – Raise your little finger and index finger at the same time. Represents devil's horns and gets you a glass of Duvel (literally 'devil' – and although it tastes like heaven, too many of these potent brews can give you a truly hellish hangover).

▼ TROLLEKELDER *Pub*
☎ 09 223 76 96; www.trollekelder.be; in
Dutch; Bij St-Jacobs 17; ⏰ 5pm-2am Mon-
Thu, 4pm-3am Fri & Sat, 4pm-2am Sun
Wide-eyed furry trolls peep out
from unlikely places throughout
this old stone-walled watering hole, such as from behind
iron-barred cells in the cave-like
cellar. Trollekelder manages to
be atmospheric without being
contrived, as evidenced by the
devoted following drinking its
blonde and dark Trollebier (troll
beer).

⭐ PLAY

Tickets for most concerts and
events are available from **Uitbureau
Gent** (☎ 09 233 77 88; Kammerstraat
19; ⏰ 9am-12.30pm & 1.30-5.30pm Mon &
Wed-Fri, 10am-12.30pm & 1.30-5.30pm Tue,
10am-12.30pm & 1.30-4.30pm Sat).

⭐ CHARLATAN *Live Music & DJs*
☎ 09 224 24 57; www.charlatan.be;
Vlasmarkt 6; ⏰ 7pm-late Tue-Sun
This stalwart bar and venue is a
local institution for live bands,
DJ sets and parties – check the
website or inhouse leaflets to see
what's on or just head on in like
everyone else.

⭐ CULTURE CLUB *Club*
☎ 09 233 09 46; www.cultureclub.be;
Afrikalaan 174; admission €8 before mid-

night, €10 after midnight; ⏰ 11pm-very
late Sat & various additional nights
This is hipster heaven, with serious
lighting and some seriously hot DJs
scratching on the decks. Check the
online calendar before trekking out
of town, and glam up for the door
police or the trip will be in vain.

⭐ HOTSY TOTSY *Jazz*
☎ 09 224 20 12; www.hotsytotsy.be;
in Dutch; Hoogstraat 1; ⏰ noon-late
Mon-Fri, 8pm-late Sat & Sun Sep-Jun,
8pm-late daily Jul & Aug
Iridescent striped wallpaper, velveteen booths and Ella Fitzgerald
et al in the background make
Hotsy Totsy a favourite haunt on
any given night, but it's posi-
tively hopping during live sessions
(usually at least Tuesdays and
Thursdays; gigs are posted on the
website). The rear room doubles
as a de facto gallery space for local
artists.

LEADING LIGHTS
Strolling around Ghent by night is dazzling thanks to its dramatically floodlit
buildings and monuments. The city's
car-free status paved the way for this,
allowing the installation of an under-
street illumination system that beams
up onto the buildings' façades (you'll
see the panels underfoot). The lighting
design continues to win international
awards.

GHENT NIGHTLIFE
Like all good student cities, Ghent is at its liveliest during semester, especially on Thursday nights. On fine evenings, hundreds of students congregate on the riverbanks of the Leie along Korenlei and Graslei, creating the vibe of a spontaneous street party. Alternative bars with regular live music and DJs line the streets around St-Jacobskerk and Vlasmarkt, while boozier student bars congregate in the university quarter (between the historic centre and Gent-St-Pieters station in the southwest). Hard beats spin at the collection of clubs at Oude Beestenmarkt, just southeast of Vlasmarkt, while the hardest of hardcore clubbers head out of the centre to internationally hyped party temples like **Culture Club** (opposite).

⭐ **SPHINX** *Cinema*
☎ 09 225 60 86; St-Michielshelling 3
This cinema specialises in art-house films.

⭐ **STUDIO SKOOP** *Cinema*
☎ 09 225 08 45; St-Annaplein 63
A five-screen cinema with a cosy, old-fashioned atmosphere.

⭐ **VLAAMSE OPERA, GENT**
Opera House
☎ 09 268 10 11; www.vlaamseopera
.be; Schouwburgstraat 3
Ghent's main opera venue was built in 1840 and boasts horse-shoe-shaped tiered balconies and elegant salons.

⭐ **VOORUIT** *Cultural Centre*
☎ 09 267 28 48; www.vooruit.be; St-Pietersnieuwstraat 23; ⏰ 11.30am-late, meals 12.30-3pm & 6-8.30pm
Everything from jazz to flamenco and book-readings to lectures takes place at this left-leaning performance, theatre, arts and cultural space. Students congregate in the vast open-plan foyer bar for coffee or drinks; you can also get hot, wholesome meals for under €8.

>SNAPSHOTS

23

Brussels, Bruges, Antwerp and Ghent are not brash, in-your-face cities. Instead, they amaze visitors (and even locals) with unsung historical treasures, underground scenes, cultural offerings and animated cafés hidden away in the backstreets. This chapter spotlights the destinations' diversity so you can tailor your trip based on your interests.

Stepping out in style in Antwerp

ACCOMMODATION

You'll find a high standard of accommodation across all price brackets throughout the four cities. Don't put too much stock in the number of stars: hotels use a Benelux classification system of one to five stars, which are awarded for objective criteria based on amenities (elevators, room service, mini bars and so on), rather than atmosphere, and don't necessarily reflect quality, location or price.

Brussels abounds with accommodation, including over 14,000 hotel rooms. Most of these are geared for midweek Eurocrats and business travellers, meaning there are often astounding deals for tourists, especially on weekends when many hotels drop their rates dramatically. Top-end hotels often charge extra for breakfast on weekdays, but throw in lavish weekend buffets. Some midrange and top-end establishments also slash their rates during the summer holidays (roughly mid-July to mid-September).

Brussels also has a growing number of B&Bs (*gastenkamers* in Dutch, *chambres d'hôtes* in French). Many B&Bs can be booked through **Bed&Brussels** (www.bnb-brussels.be), which offers various packages.

Hostels are relatively limited in Brussels, but there are a couple of excellent independents (listed opposite). There are also three HI (Hostelling International) hostels; visit www.hihostels.com.

Brussels' compactness means if you're staying anywhere in the city centre you're never far from the action – see the *Brussels Neighbourhoods* chapter for more on the individual character of each of its quarters.

Reservations can be made for free via the Brussels tourist office (p197), including online at www.brures.be, or through booking agent **Resotel** (www.belgiumhospitality.com).

Bruges is the diametric opposite of Brussels: hotels are packed and prices tend to be higher on weekends rather than weekdays. Book well ahead for high season (approximately Easter to late October) and for December's Christmas markets. Bruges' B&Bs are burgeoning and the city is also a backpacker hot spot, with more hostels than Brussels. The tourist office (p197) can book your accommodation for free.

Antwerp, in keeping with its stylish image, drips with designer B&Bs; check out www.gastenkamersantwerpen.be. The city's hostels are excellent, and more are set to open. Hotels often offer weekend reductions, especially last-minute deals, which can be booked via the tourist office (p197).

Ghent has less accommodation, especially for budget travellers, with just one hostel. There's a great B&B scene, however, organised by **Bed & Breakfast Ghent** (www.bedandbreakfast-gent.be). Book at least a month ahead if you plan to go for the Gentse Feesten (p29). The tourist office (p197) can help find accommodation.

BEST BACKPACKER BEDS

> Antwerp Backpackers Hostel, Antwerp (www.abhostel.com)
> Lybeer Travellers' Hostel, Bruges (www.hostellybeer.com)
> 2go4, Brussels (www.2go4.be)
> De Draecke, Ghent (www.vjh.be)
> Sleep Well, Brussels (www.sleepwell.be)

MOST ATMOSPHERIC B&BS

> Chambres en Ville, Brussels (www.chambresenville.be)
> B&B Phileas Fogg, Brussels (www.phileasfogg.be)
> B&B Charles Rogier XI, Antwerp (www.charlesrogierxi.be)
> B&B Huyze Hertsberge, Bruges (www.huyzehertsberge.be)
> Chambre Plus, Ghent (www.chambreplus.be)

BEST HISTORICAL TREASURES

> Hôtel Le Dixseptième, Brussels (www.ledixseptieme.be)
> Hôtel Métropole, Brussels (www.metropolehotel.com)
> Pand Hotel, Bruges (www.pandhotel.com)
> Ghent River Hotel, Ghent (www.ghent-river-hotel.be)
> Hotel 't Sandt, Antwerp (www.hotel-sandt.be)

HIPPEST DESIGNER DIGS

> The White Hotel, Brussels (www.thewhitehotel.be)
> Relais Ravestein, Bruges (www.relaisravestein.be)
> Delaneau 20, Antwerp (www.delaneau20.com)
> Monty Small Design Hotel, Brussels (www.monty-hotel.be)
> Verzameld Werk, Ghent (www.verzameldwerk.be)

ARCHITECTURE

Brussels, Bruges, Antwerp and Ghent's cross-section of architectural styles document their evolution.

Medieval architecture – the columned Romanesque and more angular Gothic – anchors each of these cities in the early chapters of their history. These styles were followed in the 16th and early-17th centuries by Flemish baroque (also known as Flemish renaissance), inspired by flamboyant trends coming out of Italy at the time. The most famous examples are the guildhalls on Brussels' Grand Place (p44), which were rebuilt in this style following the city's bombardment in 1695.

The neoclassical style of the 18th century gave way to more extravagance following Belgium's independence, with showpieces such as Brussels' Galeries St-Hubert (p48). When Léopold II took the reins in 1865, he went in for immensity best characterised by Brussels' law courts, the Palais de Justice (p60).

But it was the late 19th-century introduction of Art Nouveau that has left the most lasting mark on these four cities, especially in Brussels. Sinuous swirls, curls and floral tendrils are signature Art Nouveau motifs. Materials that supported these included wrought iron (the Eiffel Tower being the world's most famous example), glass, richly grained timbers and marble. This highly elegant style was first introduced to Brussels by

Victor Horta, whose work is showcased at his former home, the Musée Horta in Brussels (p77). Art Nouveau would have left much more of a mark had it not been for the wave of demolitions that swept Brussels in the mid-20th century. The destruction of Horta's magnificent Maison du Peuple – torn down in 1965 to make way for a bland office building – sparked international outrage, leading to the introduction of laws protecting the city's heritage. Brussels' tourist office has maps outlining an Art Nouveau trail, which can be downloaded free from its website (www .brusselsinternational.be). Antwerp also has some stunning architectural examples of the era.

After WWI even Art Nouveau innovator Victor Horta abandoned the style for the modish Art Deco, and Brussels' BOZAR (p63) is a stunning testament to the master's later work.

The country's most bizarre piece of architecture, the Atomium (p91), captures the futuristic style of the dawn of the space age.

Contemporary architecture has lagged behind (evidenced by the nondescript glass office-blocks in the EU quarter of Brussels), but a few groundbreaking buildings are rising on the skyline, such as Bruges' redbrick concert hall, the Concertgebouw (p114), and Antwerp's new Justitiepaleis (law court; p125).

One of the best ways to get up close and personal with a wide variety of Brussels' architecture is with the resident-run heritage conservation group, **Atelier de Recherche et d'Action Urbaine** (ARAU; Map pp42-3, C3; ☎ 02 219 33 45; www.arau.org; Blvd Adolphe Max 55; ☼ Apr to mid-Dec), which runs a programme of coach tours (€15) and walking tours (€10) taking you into buildings across all styles and eras that are often otherwise off-limits. Bookings can be made online through the Brussels tourist office (p197).

BEST MEDIEVAL LEGACIES
> Gravensteen, Ghent (p144)
> Belfort, Bruges (p101)
> Onze Lieve Vrouwkathedraal, Antwerp (p125)
> Hôtel de Ville, Brussels (p41)

FINEST ART NOUVEAU TREASURES
> Musée Horta, Brussels (p77)
> Old England building, Brussels (p57)
> Centre Belge de la Bande Dessinée, Brussels (p41)
> Zurenborg, Antwerp (p122)

Top left The grand façade of the Palais Royal, Brussels (p60)

ART

Like all great European cities, Brussels, Bruges, Antwerp and Ghent have a rich artistic tradition stretching back centuries. And in true Belgian style, you'll also find irreverent sculptures (p45) and comic murals (p16).

The distinction between Dutch and Flemish painters didn't come about until the late-16th century. However, artists who were commissioned in the 15th century by nobility to record their life, times and religion, and would go on to influence the direction of European art, are today known as the Flemish Primitives. They include Jan Van Eyck (c 1390–1441), whose masterpiece *The Adoration of the Mystic Lamb* (1432) resides in Ghent's St-Baafskathedraal (p145); Brussels' town painter, Van der Weyden; and Hans Memling (c 1440–94). Bruges, where many of the Flemish Primitives' works were created, harbours an outstanding collection in its Groeningemuseum (p104).

The 16th century saw Flemish painter Pieter Breugel the Elder (c 1525–67), and his two sons, Pieter the Younger (1564–1638) and Jan (1568–1625), make their mark on the artistic landscape. The two Pieters lived and worked in Brussels. Jan worked mainly in Antwerp, where he was a colleague of another famous Pieter – Belgium's most renowned painter, Pieter Paul Rubens (1577–1640). Born in Germany, Rubens returned to his parents' hometown of Antwerp and utilised both Flemish and Italian styles to create his seminal religious works and voluptuous 'Rubenesque' nudes. To keep pace with demand, he set up a studio in Antwerp where he was joined by other illustrious artists including Antoon (Anthony) Van Dyck and Jacob Jordaens.

Fauvism, cubism, symbolism and expressionism all followed, but the movement that really captured Belgium's sense of the absurd was surrealism. Two artists led the charge: René Magritte (1898–1967; p60) who played with existentialist captions ('this is not a pipe' for example, alongside a painting of one) and whose man in a bowler hat has become a national emblem; and the illusory female nudes of Paul Delvaux (1897–1994; p108).

These days there's a powerful contemporary art scene in Belgium. Look out for works by Panamarenko (1940–), whose bizarre sculptures and paintings fuse authentic and imaginary flying contraptions; Jan Fabre (1958–), famed for his Bic-art (ballpoint drawings); powerful politically themed paintings by Luc Tuymans (1958–); and Eddy Stevens (1965–), who combines elements of Rubens' lustrous realism with surrealist twists.

Final museum entry is generally 30 minutes prior to closing.

BEST RUBENS VIEWING
> Rubenshuis, Antwerp (p126)
> Onze Lieve Vrouwekathedraal, Antwerp (p125)
> Koninklijk Museum voor Schone Kunsten, Antwerp (p123)
> Rockoxhuis (p126)
> Musées Royaux des Beaux-Arts, Brussels (p60)

MOST ADVENTUROUS CONTEMPORARY ART GALLERIES
> Stedelijk Museum voor Actuele Kunst (SMAK), Ghent (p146)
> Museum van Hedendaagse Kunst Antwerpen (MuHKA), Antwerp (p125)

Top left Taking a closer look in the Musées Royaux des Beaux-Arts (p60)

DRINKING

You'll encounter a bewildering choice of Belgian beers and *jenevers* at just about every drinking establishment, but the best places to try these two famous drops are specialist 'jenever cafés' and 'beer pubs'. They almost never advertise themselves as such, so despite the tautologies (every pub serves beer, of course), we've flagged them as such throughout the Drink sections of each cities' chapter. At these specialised establishments, you'll be handed a thick menu detailing hundreds of varieties. Wading through the menus is a Herculean feat; your best bet is to ask the staff for the kind of taste and characteristics you have in mind and be guided by their expertise. For more on beer and *jenever*, see p12 and p20.

Equally bewildering is the variety of places to drink. Broadly, the term 'café' in Belgium refers to a bar or pub (although just to confuse the issue, many nightclubs call themselves 'cafés' too). Drinking establishments usually open around 10am; closing hours aren't restricted by law but simply depend on how busy it is on the night.

Cafés always serve alcohol and some, though not all, also serve food. Places that do are sometimes classified as an *eetcafé* ('eating café') or a *grand café* (a larger, more elegant version of an *eetcafé*), and it's fine to just stop in for a drink even if you're not dining. You can also just pop in for a drink at a brasserie or bistro, although these are chiefly eateries.

Anywhere that labels itself a bar generally only serves drinks. Likewise, a *herberg* (Dutch for 'tavern') is primarily a drinking spot. One of the most atmospheric cafés for drinking is the traditional *bruin café* ('brown café', sometimes called a *bruine kroeg*). So named for their wood panelling, interspersed with oversize mirrors, these small, cosy, old-fashioned pubs are prime places for mixing with locals.

If you are drinking with locals, you'll quickly notice that everyone, regardless of gender, buys rounds or risks being a social outcast. (The only person who won't be outcast is 'Bob' – the name Belgians give to a designated driver, thanks to a hugely successful campaign against drink-driving whereby drivers who pass breathaliser tests are given bright yellow 'Bob' key chains. 'Being Bob' has now become part of national parlance, and the concept is spreading across Europe.) You'll also notice locals ordering beers using a bizarre but effective kind of sign language – see p153 to learn the manoeuvres. And, of course, remember to say 'Cheers!' – in Dutch, *schol* (or *gezondheid* – to your health), and in French, *santé*!

Alas, coffee in these parts tends to pale in comparison to the cities' alcoholic beverages – see p53 – but there are an increasing number of tearooms serving aromatic, loose-leaf teas, such as Brussels' AM Sweet (p92).

BEST SPECIALIST BEER PUBS
> Bierhuis Kulminator, Antwerp (p134)
> Brugs Beertje, Bruges (p113)
> Het Waterhuis aan de Bierkant, Ghent (p152)
> 't Waagstuk, Antwerp (p136)

> Chez Moeder Lambic, Brussels (p81)

BEST JENEVER CAFÉS
> De Vagant, Antwerp (p135)
> 't Dreupelkot, Ghent (p153)

Top left These *frites* are making me thirsty

FOOD

Be sure to bring a healthy appetite with you – restaurants in Brussels, Bruges, Antwerp and Ghent dish up a seemingly endless procession of delicious fare. What's more, Belgium boasts more Michelin stars per capita than anywhere in Europe. Many cafés (ie bars or pubs) also serve meals – see p164.

Breakfast in Flanders is a hearty affair of cured meats, cheeses, cereals and so on (though never waffles at this hour). At lunchtime many restaurants offer a *dagschotel/plat du jour* (dish of the day). Also watch for a 'menu of the day' (*dagmenu* in Dutch, or *menu du jour* in French). These menus comprise three or more courses and work out cheaper than ordering individual courses à la carte. Some kitchens open as early as 6pm for dinner, but most don't get busy until at least a couple of hours later.

If Belgium has a national dish, it is mussels (*mosselen* in Dutch, *moules* in French). Forget about using a fork; use an empty shell as a pincher to prise them out. For the scoop on these much-loved molluscs see p95. Fries (*frieten* in Dutch, *frites* in French) are even more ubiquitous. Not only do they accompany mussels (and virtually any other dish), but they are easily Belgium's favourite snacks. See also 'French' Fries, p69.

Most restaurants across all price categories serve at least one or more vegetarian-friendly dishes (though vegans will find it tougher going). Salads, however, often incorporate meat or chicken, and meat stocks are regularly used in soups – check before you order. Exclusively vegetarian restaurants are thin on the ground – those included in this book are marked with a **V** symbol.

Carnivores beware: Belgians' idea of *saignant* (rare) drips with blood; *à point* (medium) is what other nationalities consider rare, and *bien cuit* is the closest you'll get to well done. (The French terms are also used by Dutch speakers.)

A great option for anyone after fast, healthy, inexpensive dishes is a new wave of Belgian chains that have fresh salads, sandwiches, vegetables, soups (some specifying that the stock is meat-free) and hot food like pies and quiches. See p96.

Sweet Belgian snacks include waffles (p51), biscuits (p49) and, of course, chocolate – see p14 and p174 for the most delectable chocolate shops.

Brussels unsurprisingly has a smorgasbord of international cuisines but you'll readily find fare from around the globe in Bruges, Antwerp and Ghent too.

For the low-down on dining with kids, see p171.

TRADITIONAL BELGIAN DISHES

You'll find dishes such as these at many restaurants throughout Flanders.

> Bloedworst – black pudding made from pig's blood, traditionally served with apple sauce
> Breugel Kop – chunks of beef and tongue set in gelatine
> Filet américain – minced beef served raw
> Konijn met pruimen – tender rabbit in prune sauce

> Paardefilet/steack de cheval – horse steak
> Paling in 't groen/anguilles-au-vert – eel in spinach sauce
> Stoemp – mashed potato topped with a sausage
> Waterzooi – creamy chicken-based stew originating in Ghent. Regional variations include Oostendse Waterzooi, a fish version from the coastal town of Ostend (p108).

Above Refuelling at L'Ultime Atome, Brussels (p80)

CINEMA

On the face, of it the Belgian love of cinema seems easily explained by two things: the fact that nightlife doesn't start until late and, of course, the climate. The country brims with cinemas, though the industry itself is underfunded compared to other art forms. An average of just two mainstream Belgian films are released per year, in addition to smaller, lower-budget independent releases.

But Belgian directors are internationally renowned, chief among them brothers Luc and Jean-Pierre Dardenne, who won the Cannes Film Festival's prestigious Palme d'Or twice – for the harrowing *Rosetta* (1999) and the rather more uplifting *L'Enfant* (2005). For an authentic slice of Antwerp life, look out for *Anyway the Wind Blows* (2003), directed by Tom Barman (frontman of Antwerp band dEUS), which follows eight interconnected characters, culminating at a party. Though not in a Belgian-directed film, Bruges recently starred on the silver screen in 2008's stylish action-comedy, *In Bruges* (p101).

Unlike its directors, Belgium's film stars generally aren't well known outside their own country, the exception being Brussels' other 'muscles', action-hero Jean-Claude Van Damme. Local stars include Vincent Grass, Natacha Amal and Matthias Schoenaerts.

In addition to multiplexes, some wonderful old-fashioned cinemas still survive; the best are listed in the Play sections of each city chapter. Brussels' Cinema Museum (p63) also screens silent films accompanied by a live pianist.

A vast array of film festivals take place each year – see p25 for details.

PERFORMING ARTS

Considering that it was an opera performance that sparked the revolution for Belgian independence (see p178), it's not surprising that the performing arts are celebrated across the country.

Brussels boasts dozens of superb venues (see the Play sections in the Brussels chapter for a cross-section of the best). But these are by no means limited to the capital. Bruges now has a state-of-the-art venue, the Concertgebouw (p114), and Antwerp has its own opera company, the Koninklijke Vlaamse Opera (p140). Antwerp is also home to the national classical ballet company, Koninklijk Ballet van Vlaanderen (p138). Catching a performance at Ghent's 1840-built opera house (p155) is a treat. There are also some charming traditional puppet theatres, notably the Théâtre Royal de Toone (p55).

Experimental theatre (in French, Dutch and sometimes English) also treads the boards, as well as edgy contemporary dance by companies such as **Rosas** (www.rosas.be) and **Ultima Vez** (www.ultimavez.com).

For performance details, check out the websites on p25. The international site www.whatsonwhen.com also links venues and events throughout Belgium. Tickets are usually available direct from the venues, or from the book/music/electronics emporium **FNAC Brussels** (Map pp42-3, D2; ☎ 02 211 40 60; www.fnac.be; City 2), **Antwerp** (Map pp120-1, C4; ☎ ticket office 0900 006 00; Grand Bazar shopping centre) and **Ghent** (Map p143, C3; ☎ 09 223 40 80; Veldstraat 88). Tickets for many events are available online through www.tickets.com. Most performing arts take a break during July and August.

Left Interesting viewing on- and off-screen at the Art Deco Arenberg Galeries, Brussels (p53)

GAY & LESBIAN

Brussels and Antwerp are Belgium's two magnets for gay and lesbian visitors, with throbbing clubs and regular parties. The most legendary is Brussels' monthly **La Démence** (www.lademence.com; p87), when bold and beautiful boys from all over Europe come to kick up their heels. Afterwards, many kick on in the five-star, fashion-themed **Royal Windsor Hôtel** (www .warwickhotels.com). The **Festival du Film Gay & Lesbien de Bruxelles** (www.fglb .org, in French) takes place in late January, while Belgian Gay & Lesbian Pride (p27) hits the streets in May.

Brussels' gay and lesbian scene is concentrated around Rue du Marché au Charbon, Rue des Pierres and Rue de la Fourche in the city's heart. In **Antwerp**, gay and lesbian hot spots (including the hyped Red & Blue, p140) are scattered across the city, and marked on the tourist office's free *Gay Antwerpen* map. Likewise, hot spots are dispersed throughout **Ghent**. Pick up the free *Gent Holebi* gay and lesbian map from Casa Rosa (p152), or buy the bimonthly booklet *Zizo* (€3.75; in Dutch but easily navigable for non-speakers). The latter is published by **Holebifoon** (☎ 0800 99 533; www.holebifoon, in Dutch), and lists dozens of venues throughout Brussels, Bruges, Antwerp and Ghent. **Bruges** doesn't have any dedicated gay and/or lesbian venues, but the tourist office keeps an updated list of gay-friendly establishments. See also the Drink and Play sections of each city chapter for venues.

Belgium is progressive about rights for same-sex couples (see p184), and checking into a double room is unlikely to pose any problems. For more infomation on Belgian attitudes towards same-sex couples, see Society & Culture, pp184–5.

KIDS

The exquisite chocolate boutiques and the comic museum might be aimed squarely at adults, but little visitors will still get a kick out of visiting these four cities. Travelling between the cities is a cinch; train journeys starting after 9am are free for kids under 12 accompanied by an adult.

Many B&Bs and hotels have baby cribs (usually costing around €15), but it's a good idea to reserve these as places often have just one on hand. Think twice about bringing a stroller to these cities, however, as you'll be wrestling it up and down endless flights of stairs and negotiating narrow footpaths and cobblestones.

Dining with kids is rarely a problem, even at top-end establishments, but you'll never see Belgian kids running amok, and will be expected to make sure that yours don't either. Restaurants often have highchairs, and sometimes special children's menus, but it's worth confirming in advance. (Even on the spur of the moment, though, it's generally easy to improvise.) With waffles and fries proliferating throughout all four cities, you may be in for a bit of arm-twisting, but kids won't go hungry.

And of course, there are plenty of kid-friendly chocolates and comics throughout these four cities, too.

BEST INDOOR ACTIVITIES FOR KIDS
> Scientastic Museum, Brussels (p47)
> Aquatopia, Antwerp (p119)
> Théâtre Royal de Toone, Brussels (p55)

BEST OUTDOOR ACTIVITIES FOR KIDS
> Cycling, all cities (p21)
> Plopsaland, near Bruges (p108)
> Mini-Europe, Brussels (p91)
> Antwerpen Zoo, Antwerp (p119)

V

SNAPSHOTS

LIVE MUSIC, DJS & CLUBBING

Whether you're in the mood to chill to the sounds of a mellow four-piece, groove to a DJ set or seriously shake it on the dance floor, these cities deliver. (OK, Bruges doesn't have any clubs to speak of, but you'll find DJs and live music.)

Jazz is far and away the style of live music you'll encounter most often, with gigs at atmospheric venues all over the cities – see p23. In Brussels, check out the **Jazzolive** (www.jazzolive.be) concert series. Blues also often get a run, with some venues, like Brussels' Bizon (p97), specialising in the genre. Rock is less common, but world music is gaining ground thanks to the multiethnic make-up of the cities. See the Diary on p25 for the best music festivals.

Look out for flyers in music shops, streetwear boutiques, bars and cafés about DJ nights, regular club fixtures and one-off parties. Online, consult www.noctis.com for funk, electro, house and clubs; www.net events.be, in Dutch and French, for general nightlife info; and www .bulexasbl.be, in French, for underground parties in Brussels. Clubbing kicks off around midnight, continuing to 5am or later, and mostly takes place at weekends in this work-hard, play-hard nation.

COOLEST JAZZ
> De Muze, Antwerp (p138)
> Sounds Jazz Club, Brussels (p81)
> L'Archiduc, Brussels (p98)
> Hotsy Totsy, Ghent (p154)

HOTTEST CLUBS
> Culture Club, Ghent (p154)
> Dirty Dancing@Mirano, Brussels (p70)
> Café d'Anvers, Antwerp (p137)
> Fuse, Brussels (p87)

PARKS & GARDENS

The cities' parks and gardens offer more than a breath of fresh air; they're also oases of art, history and culture.

The big smoke, **Brussels**, is greener than you might expect. The most popular of its central parks – attracting everyone from lunching office workers to joggers and pram-pushing parents – is the Parc de Bruxelles (p56). In the shadow of the Palais Royal and the Palais de la Nation, this gracious park was laid out in the 18th century, and was the scene of bloody fighting in 1830 during Belgium's bid for independence. Near the EU, the vast Parc du Cinquantenaire (p64) is ringed by museums. At the city's southeastern edge, the wooded parkland of the Bois de la Cambre (p76), sprawls to meet the forest of the Forêt de Soignes; while in the city's northwest, the chestnut- and magnolia-shaded Parc de Laeken (p91) extends to the Atomium. The website www.ecli.net/rbc, in French and Dutch, lists every park in the Brussels Capital Region.

Bruges has some beautiful parks lining its waterways, including one dotted with working windmills (p106).

Antwerp's main patch of green in the city is its triangular Stadspark (Map pp120–1, F6), and the western riverbank has a peaceful stretch of parkland (see p127).

Located between **Ghent's** Gent-St-Pieters station and university quarter, the leafy Citadelpark is home to both the Museum voor Schone Kunsten (p144) and the groundbreaking Stedelijk Museum voor Actuele Kunst (SMAK) (p146).

Left Speaking the international language **Above** Hide yourself in Brussels' Parc du Cinquantenaire (p64)

SHOPPING

Beer and chocolate top most shopping lists for visitors to Brussels, Bruges, Antwerp and Ghent, and the cities have an astonishing array of speciality shops for both. Other unique suitcase-stuffers include hand-made lace (p109), home-grown designer fashions (p18), classic comics (p16), diamonds (p24), and quality antiques from specialty shops, antiques fairs and markets. The cities' markets are also great for picking up clothes, music and *brocante* (bric-a-brac), and December's Christmas markets offer beautifully crafted toys, homewares and ornaments; see p22.

Also look out for the potent, alcoholic Élixir d'Anvers from Antwerp (p135), typical Bruxellois biscuits (p49), and traditional Belgian sweets (p147) and mustard (p148) from Ghent.

Bargain hunters should time their trip to Belgium for the country's two sales periods each year – starting of the first week in January, and the first week of July – for astounding discounts of up to 70%.

See p191 for an overview of standard opening hours, and p194 for a list of public holidays.

MOST ENTICING CHOCOLATE SHOPS
> Del Rey, Antwerp (p128)
> Pierre Marcolini, Brussels (p61)
> The Chocolate Line, Bruges (p107)
> Wittamer, Brussels (p62)

BEST BEER BOUTIQUES
> 2BE, Bruges (p107)
> Beermania, Brussels (p78)
> De Biertempel, Brussels (p48)

Above Hats off to a day of shopping in Galeries St-Hubert (p48)

Light and shade in the EU quarter, Brussels

BACKGROUND

HISTORY

To comprehend the country's current linguistic and cultural divisions you have to go back almost to the beginning: fragmentation first arose during Roman times, and crystallised with the formation of the Belgian state in 1831 when the nation's first constitution was drawn up in French (the country's official language at that time) by the ruling elite. It wasn't until 1898 that Dutch (locally called 'Nederlands'; or 'Vlaams', meaning 'Flemish') was recognised as a second language, and another 30 years before it was used in schools. The constitution was only published in Dutch in 1967 (even today, French is still the language of Flanders' upper class), and questions about the devolution of political power from the federal state to the regions remain unanswered. As a result, Belgium's history continues to be a work in progress.

EARLY HISTORY

Celtic and Germanic tribes are thought to have inhabited the area now known as Belgium from about 2000 BC. The Romans were the first of many to invade, first arriving in 57 BC. Julius Caesar mentioned the Belgae people during his conquest of Gaul, and when the nation needed a name following independence in 1831, the term 'Belgium' was born. Caesar's armies held Gallia Belgica for 500 years.

In the 5th century, with the Roman Empire collapsing, Germanic Franks took regional control. This change in power was the basis of Belgium's current language division – the northern region became German speaking while the southern portion remained Latin based.

THE RISE OF BRUSSELS, BRUGES, ANTWERP & GHENT

Raiding Vikings spurred the growth of feudal domains in the 9th and 10th centuries, presided over by the counts of Flanders. Baldwin the Iron Arm kicked it off by kidnapping and marrying the daughter of a French king and building a fortress in Ghent in AD 867. Over the following three centuries Baldwin's successors expanded the territory and influence of Flanders (at that time overlapping parts of present-day Belgium, France and the Netherlands) as far south as the Somme river in northern France.

As feudalism declined, the first towns rose. Flanders had been producing cloth since the 10th century, but its manufacture took off with the growth of cities like Bruges and Ghent in the 12th and 13th centuries. Merchant ships from all over Europe docked in Bruges to trade cheese, wool, lead and tin for Flemish cloth. Trade also brought coal from England, pigs from Denmark, wine from Spain, silks and oriental spices from Venice and Genoa, and furs from as far away as Russia and Bulgaria.

Because Flemish weavers relied on a steady supply of high-quality wool from England, they sided with the English during conflicts between England and France in the late 13th century. The local counts, though, were vassals of the French king and called in the French army. The situation came to a head in 1302 in bloody confrontations known as the Brugse Metten and, a few months later, the Battle of the Golden Spurs.

By the 14th century, towns including Brussels, Bruges and Ghent were all prosperous. In fact, by 1340 Ghent had grown to become the largest city in Europe after Paris.

Profound cultural changes took place during the rule of the dukes of Burgundy, starting with Philip the Good (r 1419–67), who presided from Brussels over a vast empire spanning the Burgundian region of eastern France and most of modern-day Belgium and the Netherlands, earning him the title Conditor Belgii (Belgium's founder). At the time, Philip was the richest man in Europe and at his behest Brussels' magnificent Grand Place was constructed, flanked by ornate guildhalls.

Changes were even more profound under Charles V, who was born in Ghent in 1500. At aged 15, he became Duke of Brabant and ruler of the Low Countries (this corner of northern Europe). The following year he became king of Spain and later of Naples, Sardinia, Sicily and the Spanish territories in the New World (Mexico, Peru and the Caribbean). He was crowned king of Germany and Holy Roman Emperor in 1519, becoming Europe's most powerful ruler.

Charles initially ruled from Brussels, where he was advised by the great humanist Desiderius Erasmus. He spent much of his life travelling and, later, ruling from Spain. His sister, Mary of Hungary, was responsible for the region for most of his reign, during which the Low Countries boomed.

But prosperity proved to be fickle. The great Flemish cloth towns declined due to competition from cloth manufacturers in England and the silting of the Zwin, which connected Bruges to the North Sea. In addition Charles favoured up-and-coming Antwerp over the old cloth centres. In 1555, tired of the resulting uprisings – notably in Ghent – and a lifetime of war, Charles returned to Brussels and abdicated in favour of his son Philip II. By this time Antwerp had become the region's greatest port.

RELIGIOUS DIVIDES

During Charles V's reign Protestantism swept much of Europe. The resulting religious and political rethink, the Reformation, met with severe repercussions in the Low Countries. When Charles' son Philip II came to the throne, he ruled from his native Spain, and, determined to defend the Catholic faith, he implemented a string of anti-Protestant edicts and garrisoned towns in the Low Countries with Spanish mercenaries. In 1566 the Protestants revolted, and Philip retaliated with a force of 10,000 troops.

In the turbulent years that followed – the Revolt of the Netherlands – the present-day borders of Belgium, Luxembourg and the Netherlands were roughly drawn. The Netherlands expelled the Spaniards, while Belgium and Luxembourg, known then as the Spanish Netherlands, stayed under southern rule.

Brussels was proclaimed capital of the Spanish Netherlands in 1585 and thousands of Protestants were forced to move north to the Netherlands.

In 1598 Philip II handed the Spanish Netherlands to his daughter Infanta Isabella and her husband, Archduke Albert of Austria. Their flamboyant 40-year reign gave rise to new industries like lace making and diamond processing. In turn, this brief economic boom boosted cultural life in Brussels and Antwerp and brought to the fore great painters, such as Pieter Paul Rubens.

Antwerp's glory days were cut short by the Treaty of Westphalia, signed in 1648, which closed part of the Scheldt river to all non-Dutch ships, triggering the city's collapse.

With many of its skilled workers gone, much of the Spanish Netherlands sunk into poverty. Meanwhile the newly formed Jesuit order prospered and multiplied, and elaborate baroque churches were built in the region as symbols of the Catholic Church's power.

French plans to dominate Europe meant many wars were fought in this buffer land. Fighting came to a head with the War of Spanish Succession (1701–13), which saw the Spanish Netherlands handed to the Austrians.

THE SEEDS OF BENELUX

The mighty Austrian Hapsburgs ruled from 1713 to 1794. Brussels was the base for central control but the Austrians allowed the country a large degree of independence.

After yet another battle in 1794, the French reclaimed the region and the following year absorbed it into France. French laws were ushered in, the Catholic Church was repressed (many churches were ransacked and monasteries closed) and deeply unpopular conscription was introduced.

A fundamental turning point came in 1815 when Napoleon Bonaparte, leader of the new French state, was defeated at the Battle of Waterloo near Brussels. This resulted in the Congress of Vienna and the creation of the United Kingdom of the Netherlands, which incorporated the Netherlands, Belgium and Luxembourg – the precursor to the Benelux (*Be*lgium, *Ne*therlands, *Lux*embourg) economic and political alliances that exist today (an example of this tri-nation cooperation is Benelux's bid for the 2018 FIFA World Cup).

The United Kingdom of the Netherlands was created largely to pre-serve the balance of power in Europe and ignored the fact that it forced together people of different religions and customs.

During this period, William of Orange-Nassau, crowned King William I in Brussels, divided his time equally between Brussels and the new kingdom's twin capital, the Hague. But William made enemies quickly after refusing to give southern Belgium fair political representation and trying to impose Dutch as the national language. The latter an-gered not only the French-speaking Walloons in the south of Belgium but also Dutch speakers in the north who regarded their Flemish language as distinct from the Dutch spoken in the Netherlands (see also p193).

The inevitable Belgian revolution began dramatically during an opera performance in Brussels on 25 August 1830. The opera – about Naples' uprising against the Spanish two centuries earlier – inspired the mainly bourgeois audience to join the workers demonstrating outside against the Dutch rulers. Together, the opera-goers and the workers stormed the town hall, and a new nation would soon be born.

BELGIAN INDEPENDENCE

At the Conference of London in January 1831, Belgium was officially declared a neutral state. On 21 July 1831 Léopold of Saxe-Coburg Gotha (uncle of future British monarch Queen Victoria), became King Léopold I of Belgium. The country now celebrates his coronation as its annual 21 July National Day holiday. King Léopold oversaw the industrial revolu-tion in Wallonia in particular, where coal mines and iron-making factories took off. The ensuing years saw the start of Flemish nationalism, with tension growing between Dutch speakers and French speakers that would eventually lead to the language partition that continues to divide the country.

Léopold II (r 1865–1909) came to the throne on his father's death. He was committed to transforming the tiny country into a strong nation, both through national development and colonial conquests. In 1885, Léopold personally acquired a huge slice of central Africa – an area 70 times larger than Belgium. Over the following 25 years, millions of Congolese died due to legally permitted atrocities committed by Belgian trade during Léopold's rule. In 1908 the king was stripped of his possession, although the Belgian state held on to the Congo until 1960.

WWI, WWII & BEYOND

When war broke out in 1914, Germany violated Belgian neutrality and occupied the country. After the war the Treaty of Versailles abolished Belgium's neutral status and the country was given reparations from Germany. In 1934 Léopold II's nephew and successor, Albert I (r 1909–34) died in a rock-climbing accident; he was succeeded by his son, Léopold III (r 1934–51).

In 1940 the Germans launched a surprise air attack on the Netherlands, Belgium and Luxembourg and within eight days Belgium was occupied and quickly surrendered to the Germans. The Belgian government opposed the king's decision to surrender and fled to London where it operated in exile throughout WWII. Belgium and Luxembourg were liberated in September 1944.

After WWII the country was caught up in a constitutional crisis over Léopold III's wartime actions. In 1951, under pressure from Walloon socialists, he abdicated in favour of his son Baudouin I (r 1951–93), who succeeded in bringing the nation together. His fair treatment of the Flemish and Walloons earned him respect from both sides. When he died suddenly in 1993, Baudouin was succeeded by his younger brother, the present King Albert II (b 1934–).

Belgium emerged as a key player in international politics after WWII. In 1958 Brussels became the provisional seat of the European Commission and the Council of Ministers, the executive and decision-making bodies of today's EU. In 1967 the North Atlantic Treaty Organisation (NATO) moved to Brussels from France a year after the French withdrew from NATO's military wing. A new NATO headquarters, being built on the northeastern outskirts of the capital, is expected to be finished in 2009.

GOVERNMENT & POLITICS

There's a saying in Belgium that people have more chance of becoming a minister than they do of winning the lottery, and statistically it's probably true. The government was decentralised in 1993 resulting in three regional governments representing Flanders, Wallonia and the Brussels Capital Region, in line with the communities' demands for linguistic, territorial and cultural autonomy. That means that, despite its diminutive population (and despite being a constitutional hereditary monarchy, led by its sovereign), Belgium has no fewer than six separate governments and six parliaments, with Federal, Regional and Linguistic Community divisions. Regions have responsibility for territorial affairs, such as roads and infrastructure, while linguistically defined communities look after personal designations like education, and the federal government is responsible for defence, finance and the judiciary. Voting is compulsory by law for all Belgian citizens.

The regions, however, are very different entities. While Wallonia's economy rode on the back of the steel and iron-ore industries until their slump in the 1970s, Flanders surged ahead, bolstered by information technology and tourism industries. This has been one of the driving forces for calls for the separation of Wallonia and Flanders. Some people in Flanders resent that their taxes are footing the bill for Wallonia's economic shortfalls. (Taxes are an especially sensitive issue in Belgium, given that they're among the highest in the world.) However, because Flanders has a larger ageing population than Wallonia's, at the same time as Wallonia's technology industries are picking up, this subsidisation may be reversed within the next generation.

RULING COALITIONS

Not only does Belgium have numerous parliaments, it also has numerous political parties (with Dutch-speaking and Francophone versions). These parties form ruling coalitions as most are too small to rule outright. Belgium was long governed by an ever-changing coalition headed by the Christian (Catholic) Democrats. In 1999 voters opted for an unusual coalition of Liberals, Socialists and Greens, led by Guy Verhofstadt, the first Liberal (commonly defined as pro-business) prime minister in 50 years.

The Socialists and Liberals renewed their coalition in 2003, with Verhofstadt as leader. In addition to the major players, there are numerous minor parties, including the extreme right-wing party Vlaams Blok. It won

20% of the popular vote in Flanders and 10% of the national vote in 2003, but was later banned on grounds of racism. The party changed its name to Vlaams Belang and although it garnered support at local elections in Flanders in late 2006, there was an 8.5% swing away from the party. It poses an obstacle for Flemish people who support an independent Flanders, but don't support Vlaams Belang's ideals. Vlaams Belang also poses a problem for many residents, especially in Antwerp, the party's headquarters, where people fear that they are perceived as intolerant as a result of the party's publicity. In reality Vlaams Belang only represent an extreme minority, and to counter negative perceptions, residents have erected signs along many of Antwerp's streets reading *Zonder Haat Straat* (Street Without Hate).

The country's linguistic and cultural divisions reached breaking point following the June 2007 national election. Despite victory over Verhofstadt's coalition, the Christian Democratic & Flemish Party/New-Flemish Alliance (CD&V/N-VA), headed by centre-right leader Yves Leterme, was unable to negotiate forming a new coalition government. In essence, this was because the main parties were profoundly divided over how much power to devolve to the two respective regions. Leterme needed at least three coalition partners for a parliamentary majority, which meant shoring up support among opposing linguistic and ideological quarters. That support eluded him. For over half-a-year, Belgium was without a federal government.

CRISES & CONUNDRUMS

With economic issues piling up, including the need for a national budget to fund services, in mid-December 2007, King Albert asked outgoing prime minister, Guy Verhofstadt, to form a caretaker coalition government

LIFE IMITATING ART?

Francophone public broadcaster RTBF interrupted normal programming in December 2006 with footage of a reporter outside the Royal Palace in Brussels, claiming that Flanders had declared independence and King Albert had left the country. Only after half an hour did the programme makers admit it was a hoax. Although many were appalled about being hoodwinked (an RTBF survey shows 89% of viewers believed the report), the station stated that it intended to demonstrate the importance of the ongoing political debate for the future of Belgium. Sure enough, 2007's election fallout occurred just six months later, and the debate continues today.

through to March 2008. That month, power transferred to a longer-term coalition, and Leterme replaced Verhofstadt as prime minister, moving to begin negotiations on devolution. Achieving agreement across the linguistic divide on constitutional change, however, is still a major challenge.

A symbolic but significant concern that highlights the crisis is the Brussels Capital Region's bilingual voting constituency. The constituency encompasses the mostly French-speaking city of Brussels, but also adjoining Flemish (Dutch-speaking) communes. All sides of Flemish politics want these Flemish areas to become part of the neighbouring Flemish constituencies and for Brussels to remain a separate unit. On the flip side, the French-speaking parties are adamant that keeping the constituency bilingual will protect French speakers who live in these Flemish areas (bearing in mind that in the event of a split, any French speakers in these areas would only have the option of voting for Dutch-speaking candidates).

LOOKING AHEAD

Although the recent political crisis has abated, the question of whether Belgium will hold together or split is never far away. Brussels, with its geographical location in Flanders, its primary linguistic orientation in Wallonia, and its EU capital status, is the major sticking point. There is also the question of what would happen to Belgium's tiny German-speaking region. A further question arises over Belgium's monarchy, although many younger Belgians (and many tax payers in general) believe a monarchy is unnecessary in the 21st century.

If Belgium did split, it's unlikely that Wallonia would join France, or that Flanders would join the Netherlands (despite surveys of Dutch citizens that overwhelmingly support Flanders becoming part of their country). Instead, one model for the future that's often bandied about is that Flanders and Wallonia would each become independent, and Brussels would become its own city-state (in the same vein as Singapore), possibly even administered by the EU. Certainly, the economic and legal unification provided by the EU makes it more viable than at any other time in modern history for such small nations to exist independently.

But the general sentiment in most quarters is that people don't want Belgium to split. Aside from personal attachment, a key pragmatic reason is that 'Belgian' has become a trademark, with considerable international standing as a byword for quality (such as 'Belgian chocolate' or 'Belgian beer'). Some people feel this reputation may be diminished if Flanders and Wallonia split into separate countries since these are lesser-known names internationally.

For the foreseeable future at least, it seems likely that Belgium will endure.

SOCIETY & CULTURE

'Nothing works here, and still it works. That's Belgium.' Statements by locals such as this sum up Belgians' acceptance of – even pride about – their country's seeming absurdity at times (the fact that it ticked along quite nicely without a federal government for six months, for example). A similar sentiment you'll hear is that 'there's always a solution'. Belgians are on the whole an innovative, optimistic bunch, with an easy-going outlook on life.

Belgians often identify themselves as Flemish (those that speak Dutch) or Walloon (those that speak French) first, and Belgian second. Additionally, all four cities, but especially Brussels, Antwerp and Ghent, are vibrant hubs of multiculturalism, whose populations include many other European nationalities, along with Moroccans, Turks and Africans (particularly immigrants from the former Belgian Congo).

Religion also plays a part in identity and day-to-day life including politics and education. Roughly 75% of Belgium's population is Roman Catholic, and despite church attendance plummeting in the late-20th century (only 3% of the Flemish population goes to church weekly), traditions endure. Protestant communities also maintain a strong presence. Antwerp is home to the country's largest Jewish community, and Brussels and Antwerp also have sizable Muslim populations.

When it comes to moral freedom, Belgium is a world leader. Same-sex couples have been able to wed legally in Belgium since 2003, and have the same rights as heterosexuals, including inheritance and adoption

MIND YOUR LANGUAGE

It's important to note that Bruges, Antwerp and Ghent are emphatically Flemish and therefore Dutch-speaking. Hence, visitors' attempts to speak French here aren't appreciated. English, on the other hand, is considered neutral and, as the international lingua franca, is much more commonly used. In Brussels, French is the main day-to-day language, so it's fine to speak in French, though English is widely spoken.

(although in practice few gay couples adopt, due to the difficulty of obtaining authorisation by overseas authorities as there are few Belgian babies up for adoption). Euthanasia was legalised in 2002, and the country has been a vocal critic of the war in Iraq.

For all its quirks and contrasts, Belgium is a refreshingly uncomplicated place in terms of social interaction, with few pitfalls for visitors. The main one to watch out for is language; see boxed text opposite. A couple of others: men and women, and women and women, greet each other with three kisses on the cheek (starting on the left) when meeting for the first time; after that it's usually just one kiss (again on the left cheek). Men always shake hands with men. And, unlike in neighbouring France and the Netherlands, shopkeepers generally won't greet you when you enter their premises. This isn't unfriendliness, but to avoid being seen as giving the hard sell – something that's shunned by Belgians, who are unassuming and modest by nature and don't blow their own trumpet. But contrasts are ever-present: one of the national symbols is Brussels' Manneken Pis (p44), unabashedly baring himself to the world.

LINGUISTIC DIVIDES

Language plays an intrinsic role in shaping Belgian society, culture and politics. The decision in 1962 to cut the country in half with an invisible line known as the 'linguistic divide' created the regions of Flanders, Wallonia and bilingual Brussels. The country's present population of 10.5

LANGUAGES SPOKEN IN BELGIUM
- Dutch
- French
- German
- French & Dutch

FLANDERS ⊛ **Brussels**

WALLONIA

BACKGROUND

million people is split between Dutch-speaking Flanders (Vlaanderen in Dutch) in the north with 60% of the population, French-speaking Wallonia (la Wallonie in French) in the south with 27%, and the German-speaking eastern cantons in Belgium's far east, comprising 13% of the population (see p185). Although Brussels is geographically in Flanders (and although it's officially bilingual), it is primarily French-speaking.

See also the boxed text on p184 and p193 for more on language, including a list of phrases in Dutch and French.

FURTHER READING

The Art of Being Belgian (Richard Hill, 2005) On-the-money and very witty account of the country's idiosyncrasies by this British author living in Belgium for some 40 years.

De Leeuw van Vlaanderen (The Lion of Flanders; Hendrik Conscience, 1838) Stirring epic about the Flemish Battle of the Golden Spurs revolt against France that sheds light on today's divide.

Good Beer Guide to Belgium (Tim Webb, first published 1992) A specialist 'travel guide' for dedicated beer enthusiasts.

Great Beers of Belgium (Michael Jackson, first published 1998) The definitive tome of Belgian beers, by the beer writer (not the entertainer), Michael Jackson, who is considered by many to be the best in his field.

Flemish & Dutch Paintings (Edited by RH Fuchs, 1997) Traces the development of pivotal artistic movements.

Het Verdriet van België (The Sorrow of Belgium; Hugo Claus, 1983) Poignant coming-of-age novel by Flemish writer Claus depicting Nazi collaboration during WWII Belgium through the eyes of a Flemish adolescent.

History of the Low Countries (Edited by JCH Blom, 1999) Extensive and incisive documentation of the region's very complex history.

A Tall Man in a Low Land: Some Time Among the Belgians (Harry Pearson, 1999) Hilarious and informative travelogue packed with observations about Belgium's more surreal aspects.

Tintin: The Complete Companion (Michael Farr, 2001) Detailed behind-the-scenes look at Hergé and his cub reporter's adventures.

DIRECTORY
TRANSPORT
ARRIVAL & DEPARTURE
AIR

The main international touch-down zone is **Brussels International Airport** (BRU; Zaventem Airport; Map pp8-9; ☎ 02 753 77 53; www.brusselsairport .be), located 13km northeast of the city centre. Brussels' second airport, **Brussels South Charleroi Airport** (CRL; Map pp8-9; ☎ 07 125 12 11; www.charleroi-airport.com), is 46km southeast of the city and is used mainly by budget airlines including Ryanair.

The small **Antwerp Airport** (ANR; Map pp8-9; www.antwerp-airport.be) is 4km southeast of the city and has limited flights to and from London City airport and Manchester, plus Innsbruck, Austria in winter. The airport is served by buses.

Brussels International Airport

From the train station located on Level 1 of the terminal building, the **Brussels Airport Express** (☎ 02 528 28 28, select option 4 for English) runs up to four times an hour from 5.26am, with the last train leaving at 12.26am (5.17am and 11.50pm respectively on weekends) to Brussels' Gare du Nord (18 minutes), Gare Centrale (22 minutes) and Gare du Midi (30 minutes). The trip costs €4.40/2.90 one way (1st/2nd class). Private company **MIVB/STIB** (☎ 02 515 20 00; www.stib.be) runs express buses (line 12 on weekdays, line 11 on weekends) from the airport to Schuman metro station and from there to Gare Bruxelles-Luxembourg. The service runs regularly from 7am to 8pm (outside these hours and on weekends Schuman is the last stop) taking roughly 30 minutes; current timetables are posted online.

AIR TRAVEL ALTERNATIVES

To save the environment (and, often, save time and/or costs too), consider these alternatives to air travel:

> Train – The **Eurostar** (p188) is now carbon-neutral for passengers and a stellar option for crossing the Channel. Within continental Europe, long-haul trains converge on Brussels with connections to Bruges, Antwerp and Ghent – see p188. The info-packed website www.seat61.com has advice.

> Ferry – **P&O** (www.poferries.com) sails overnight from Zeebrugge, Belgium to Hull, England (14 hours), while **Superfast Ferries** (www.superfast.com) sails overnight three times per week between Zeebrugge and Rosyth, Scotland (18 hours).

> Bus – See p189 for international bus information.

CLIMATE CHANGE & TRAVEL

Travel – especially air travel – is a significant contributor to global climate change. At Lonely Planet, we believe that all who travel have a responsibility to limit their personal impact. As a result, we have teamed with Rough Guides and other concerned industry partners to support Climate Care, which allows people to offset the greenhouse gases they are responsible for with contributions to energy-saving projects and other climate-friendly initiatives in the developing world. Lonely Planet offsets all staff and author travel.

For more information, turn to the responsible travel pages on www.lonelyplanet .com. For details on offsetting your carbon emissions and a carbon calculator, go to www .climatecare.org.

Tickets cost €3. **De Lijn** (www.delijn.be, in Dutch) also runs a bus between the airport and Gare du Nord, but the Brussels Airport Express (p187) is much faster.

A taxi to central Brussels will cost around €35.

Brussels South Charleroi Airport

A flat fare of €10.50 will get you from any train station in Belgium to Charleroi South station, from where bus line A or line 68 transport you to the airport in around five minutes (the bus ticket is included in the flat fare).

Buses to the airport (€11/20 one-way/return; one hour) are based around flight departure times and leave Brussels' Gare du Midi just over two hours before departures. Buses to Gare du Midi leave around half an hour after flight arrivals.

The airport also has direct bus services to Bruges four times per day (€20/38 one-way/return; two hours).

Antwerp Airport

Antwerp is connected to the airport by **express buses** (☎ 32 52 33 40 00; €10). These depart from the airport from 5am (7am Sun) to midnight; they leave Antwerp from 4am (6am Sun) with the last departure at 11pm. The journey takes 50 minutes. All buses leave the airport from level 0.

TRAIN

National train services are managed by **Belgian railways** (www.b-rail .be; ☎ 02 528 28 28; ☺ customer service 8am-6pm), easily identified by its logo of a 'B' in an oval. There are four levels of service: InterCity (IC) trains, which are the fastest; InterRegional (IR) trains; local (L) trains; and peak-hour (P) commuter services stopping at specific stations. There's usually an IC or IR train departing every half-hour to an hour from Brussels to major Belgian destinations including Antwerp, Bruges and Ghent. Each of Brussels' main stations – Gare du Nord, Gare Centrale and Gare du Midi – has an information office. Although Gare du Midi translates from the French as 'mid station', its Dutch name, Zuid (South) more accurately describes its location, and it's important not to confuse Gare du Midi with Gare Centrale (Central Station).

Gare du Midi (Map p81, A4) is Brussels' main station for international travel. **Thalys** (www.thalys .com) operates high-speed trains connecting Brussels, Bruges, Antwerp, Ghent and other Belgian cities to destinations in France, the Netherlands and Germany – see the table below for estimated travel times between cities. **Société Nationale des Chemins de Fer Luxembourgeois** (CFL; www.cfl.lu) links Luxembourg City with Brussels' Gare du Nord (Map p69) in three hours. Check the website for details.

Geographically, London is closer to Brussels than it is to northern British cities, and the highly civilised **Eurostar** (www.eurostar .com) whisks you between Brussels' Gare du Midi and central London's St Pancras International Station in just one hour, 51 minutes (one hour, 46 minutes between Brussels and Ebbsfleet International in Kent). Direct Eurostar services also connect Brussels and Lille, France, in 34 minutes. The 'Latest Deals' section of Eurostar's website often has bargains.

BUS

Trains are invariably faster and more comfortable but Brussels, Bruges, Antwerp and Ghent are also well connected to the rest of Europe (including the UK) with

Train Travel Times

	🚉 Antwerp	🚉 Bruges	🚉 Brussels	🚉 Ghent
Amsterdam	2hr	4hr	2hr 30min	3hr
Antwerp	–	1hr 20min	35min	45min
Bruges	1hr 20min	–	1hr	25min
Brussels	35min	1hr	–	40min
Cologne	3hr 30min	3hr 45min	2hr 15min	3hr 15min
Ghent	45min	25min	40min	–
Paris	2hr	2hr 30min	1hr 30min	2hr 10min

inexpensive buses operated by **Eurolines** (www.eurolines.com). Tickets can be booked on the website.

VISAS

There are no entry requirements or restrictions on EU nationals visiting Belgium. Citizens of Australia, Canada, Israel, Japan, New Zealand and the USA do not need visas to visit the country as tourists for up to three months. Except for people from a few other European countries (such as Norway), everyone else must have a visa – check with Belgium's **Ministry of Foreign Affairs** (www.diplomatie.be) for info.

GETTING AROUND

In the Brussels Neighbourhoods chapter of this book, the nearest metro station (Ⓜ) or *premetro* station (🚊) is noted at the end of each listing. Where a tram is closer than either of these, the route number is indicated after the 🚊 symbol. Route maps can be downloaded from www.stib.be, or picked up from the tourist office. See also the transport map on the pull-out map with this book.

The town centres of Bruges, Antwerp and Ghent are all compact enough to be seen on foot, but all three have buses, and Antwerp and Ghent also have good tram networks. Train stations and tourist offices in each city can provide you with transport maps.

Single-trip public transport tickets in each city are generally good for one hour after validation, but check when you purchase them for exceptions.

All four cities are ideal to explore on two wheels and bicycle rental averages around €10 per day.

PUBLIC TRANSPORT

Brussels has an extensive, efficient and easy-to-use public transport system, comprising the ultrareliable metro, trams, the *premetro* (trams that go underground for part of their journey) and buses. Public transport generally runs from 5.30am to 11pm or midnight daily. Noctis night buses, managed by MIVB/STIB (p187) run between midnight and 3am Friday and Saturday nights. Tickets allowing access to all forms of public transport in Brussels are available from vending machines in metro stations, from STIB kiosks and some newsagents, and on buses and trams. The best travel pass for visitors doing the sights is the Brussels Card (p192).

A single-journey ticket on public transport costs €2 on board or €1.50 if purchased beforehand; five/10-journey tickets cost €6.70/11. Day tickets (€4) are great value if you'll be jumping on and off public transport all day. Night buses cost €3 per single journey, €7 for a night pass, or €21 for 10 trips. Validate your ticket at the start of your trip in the machines located at the entrance to metro platforms, or inside buses and trams. For a taxi, call **Taxis Bleus** (☎ 02 268 00 00).

Buses operate in **Bruges** but the only place you're likely to need one is from the train station (Map pp102–3, B8) to the city centre (board any bus marked 'Centrum'). A single fare is €1.50 if bought on the bus, or €1.20 if bought from ticket machines; multitrip tickets are available. Taxis are generally waiting at the bus station and the Markt (Map pp102–3, C5). To book a taxi in Bruges, phone ☎ 050 33 44 44.

Antwerp has a good network of buses, trams and *premetro*. Tickets are €1.50 onboard or €1.20 if purchased from machines; multi-trip tickets are available. You can usually find a taxi at Groenplaats (Map pp120–1, C4) and outside Centraal Station (Map pp120–1, H5), otherwise call **Antwerp Taxi** (☎ 03 238 38 38).

Ghent has two train stations. The main one, Gent-St-Pieters, is about 2km south of the city centre, but regularly connected by trams 1, 10 and 11. Some trains also stop at Gent-Dampoort to the east of the city; served by buses 3, 17, 18, 38 and 39. Public transport tickets are €1.50 onboard (though this is sometimes refused if there's

BRUSSELS ON WHEELS
A fantastic new initiative by the City of Brussels, **Cyclocity** (www.cyclocity.be) lets you buy a subscription card (€1.50 per week), then rent a bike (€0.50 for the first half-hour, and €0.50 for every hour after that; charged to your credit card) from any of its 23 centrally located stations. Afterwards, simply return it to any station in the network.

a machine at the tram stop), or €1.20 from machines; multitrip tickets are available. Call ☎ 09 333 33 33 for a taxi.

BIKE RENTAL
See Brussels on Wheels above for cycle hire in **Brussels**.

In **Bruges**, bikes can be rented from the **train station** (Map pp102-3, B8; ☎ 050 30 23 29).

For bike hire in **Antwerp**, try **Freewieler** (Map pp120-1, B2; ☎ 03 213 22 51; www.v-zit.be, in Dutch; Steenplein).

In **Ghent**, rent bikes either from the train station (Map p143, A6) or from **Biker** (Map p143, D1; ☎ 09 224 29 03; Steendam 16).

PRACTICALITIES
BUSINESS HOURS
Generally, restaurants open for lunch from 11.30am or noon until 2pm or 3pm. Dinner service starts at about 6.30pm or 7pm, and goes to 10pm or 11pm. Brasseries

usually open from 11am until midnight or 1am. Most cafés are open by 10am or 11am, and some will still be going at 5am; closing times usually depend on how busy a place is on any given night.

Banks open from 8.30am or 9am and close between 3.30pm and 5pm Monday to Friday. Some close for an hour at lunch, and many also open Saturday mornings. Post offices generally operate from 9am to 5pm Monday to Friday and until noon Saturday. Smaller branches close for lunch and larger ones stay open until 6pm.

Shops usually open from 9am or 10am until 6pm or 7pm, Monday to Saturday, and some also open on Sunday.

DISCOUNTS

Many of Belgium's attractions and entertainment venues offer discounts for students and children, though family rates are rare. Students will need to produce an International Student Identity Card (ISIC) to qualify for reduced admission to museums and other sights, and for discount cinema tickets and train fares. Senior citizens and travellers with disabilities will generally receive a discount.

If you're planning some serious sightseeing, you'll save a bundle with the **Brussels Card** (www.bitc.be), which can be ordered online prior to your visit. For €20 a day or €33 for three days you get access to 25 museums, bus, tram and train transport in the city, and discounts in bars and restaurants. Aimed at young travellers (under 26 years, though there's no official limit) is the **Manneken Pass** (www.mannekenpass .eu; €5) which includes access to all of Brussels' public transport networks for one day, plus various freebies and discounts. Both can be picked up from Brussels' tourist offices (p197) on the Grand Place or at the Brussels Midi Station.

ELECTRICITY

Plugs in Belgium have two round pins. Voltage is 220V AC; frequency 50Hz. Appliances rated US 110V need a transformer to work safely.

EMERGENCIES

While the rate of violent crime in Belgium is low compared with many European countries, petty theft does occur, more so in large cities. Pickpocket haunts in Brussels include the Grand Place, the narrow streets around Ilôt Sacré, Rue Neuve, and the markets at Gare du Midi and Place du Jeu-de-Balle.

Ambulance/Fire Brigade (☎ 100)
Police (☎ 101)
Helpline (☎ 02 648 40 14) Twenty-four-hour helpline based in Brussels.
SOS Viol (☎ 02 534 36 36) Rape crisis line in Brussels.

LANGUAGE

Belgium's three official languages are Dutch, French and German – see the language map p185 . In all four cities visitors can get by with English most of the time, but if you do speak the local lingo, be sure not to commit the faux pas of using the wrong one (see p184).

You may hear people calling the Dutch spoken in Belgium 'Flemish', thereby underlining the cultural identity of the Flemish people. In reality, grammar and spelling rules of Dutch in Belgium and Dutch in the Netherlands are the same, and 'Flemish' is not a separate language in itself. Speech is a slightly different matter: Dutch spoken in Belgium utilises softer pronunciations and there are a few words and phrases typical to the region. In all, however, Dutch and Flemish people are perfectly intelligible to each other. Flanders' dialects vary from city to city, though visitors are unlikely to encounter these. For more about the Dutch language, check out the free brochure downloadable at http://taalunieversum.org/taalunie/publicaties/brochureeng.pdf (in English). See also p185–6.

Below, Dutch phrases are given first, followed by the French. For more extensive language coverage get a copy of Lonely Planet's *Dutch Phrasebook*, or *Small Talk Western Europe*.

USEFUL PHRASES

Hello.	*Dag/Hallo.*	*Bonjour.*
Goodbye.	*Dag.*	*Au revoir.*
Yes./No.	*Ja./ Nee.*	*Oui./Non.*
Please.	*Alstublieft.*	*S'il vous plaît.*
Thank you (very much).	*Dank u (wel).*	*Merci (beaucoup).*
That's fine/You're welcome.	*Graag gedaan.*	*Je vous en prie.*
Excuse me.	*Excuseer mij.*	*Excusez-moi.*
I'm sorry.	*Pardon.*	*Pardon.*
Do you speak English?	*Spreekt u Engels?*	*Parlez-vous anglais?*
I don't understand.	*Ik begrijp het niet.*	*Je ne comprends pas.*
A beer, please.	*Een bier, alstublieft.*	*Une bière, s'il vous plaît.*
I'm a vegetarian.	*Ik ben vegetariër.*	*Je suis végétarien/ végétarienne.* (m/f)
That was delicious!	*Dat was heerlijk!*	*C'était délicieux!*
I'd like to buy...	*Ik wil graag...kopen.*	*Je voudrais acheter...*
How much is it?	*Hoeveel is het?*	*C'est combien?*
I'm ill.	*Ik ben ziek.*	*Je suis malade.*
Call (a doctor/ the police)!	*Haal (een doktor/ de politie)!*	*Appelez (un médecin/ la police)!*

HOLIDAYS
New Year's Day 1 January
Easter Monday March/April
Labour Day 1 May
Ascension Day 40th day after Easter
Whit Monday 7th Monday after Easter
Festival of the Flemish Community 11 July
Belgium National Day 21 July
Assumption Day 15 August
All Saints' Day 1 November
Armistice Day 11 November
Christmas Day 25 December

INTERNET
INTERNET CAFÉS
Internet cafés are relatively thin on the ground in these cities. Prices vary from €0.50 to €1.50 for 15 minutes, to €1 to €5 per hour. An increasing number of hotels and hostels and some cafés and bars offer wi-fi.

Try these internet cafés:
2Zones (Map pp120-1, C3; ☎ 03 232 24 00; Wolstraat 15, Antwerp; ⊗ 11am-midnight)
Coffeelounge (Map p143, C2; ☎ 09 329 39 11; Botermarkt 9, Ghent; ⊗ 10am-7pm Wed-Mon)
Coffee Link (Map pp102-3, C6; ☎ 050 34 99 73; Mariastraat 38, Bruges; ⊗ 11am-6pm Thu-Tue)
Dotspot (Map pp40-1, C6; ☎ 02 513 61 03; Rue du Lombard 83, Place St-Jean, Brussels; ⊗ 10.15am-2pm & 2.30-6pm Mon-Sat)

USEFUL WEBSITES
Belgian Beer Board (http://belgianbeer board.com) Guaranteed to make you thirsty, with up-to-date info on everything beer related.

Belgium Online in English (www.xpats .com) Belgium's international community provide loads of insider information, including local news in English and an entertainment agenda.
Belgian Tourist Office (www.visitbelgium .com) Events listings and comprehensive country-wide information.
BrusselsLife (www.brusselslife.be) Comprehensive info about the capital – from restaurants to clubs and more.
Lonely Planet (www.lonelyplanet.com) Information, links and resources.
Use-it (www.use-it.be) Irreverent, info-crammed free downloadable maps for Brussels, Bruges, Antwerp and Ghent produced by young locals.

MONEY
ATMS
Many ATMs won't accept PIN codes with more than four digits – ask your bank for advice before you leave.

CHANGING MONEY
There are exchange bureaus (*wisselkantoren* in Dutch, *bureaux d'échange* in French) at airports or train stations as well as major tourist precincts. Ever-fewer establishments accept travellers' cheques.

COSTS
Shoestringers staying in hostels, hitting a museum, filling up on *frites* and baguettes and downing a good beer or two can expect to spend from €40 per day. If you go

for hotels with full amenities and midrange restaurants, count on paying upwards of €120 per day. Of course, with all those antiques, designer fashions and diamonds, the sky's the limit.

CREDIT CARDS

Visa is the most widely accepted credit card, followed by Master-Card. American Express and Diners Club cards are only accepted at the more exclusive establishments. Some restaurants still don't accept credit cards.

A computer-chip credit card with a PIN is required for many automated services, such as Brussels' Cyclocity bicycle hire outlets (p191) as well as train ticket machines. Note that many North American Visas and MasterCards don't yet have computer-chip and PIN technology and international computer-chip cards don't always work for these automated services. Check with your credit card provider for advice.

ORGANISED TOURS

To see Brussels or Antwerp from the inside out with local residents, see Insider Information, p60.

BRUSSELS
Architectural tours (see p160).
Brussels by Water (☎ 02 203 64 06; www .scaldisnet.be; Ave du Port; 45-min port tours adult/concession from €4/3; ☼ 2pm, 3pm,

4pm & 5pm Tue, Wed & Sun May-Sep) Brussels' canals offer an interesting (if industrial) perspective of the capital.
Pro Velo (☎ 02 502 73 55; www.provelo .org; Rue de Londres 15; tours from €8) Arranges good self-guided bicycle tours.

BRUGES
Canal cruises (€6.50 for a 30-min tour; ☼ 10am-6pm, Nov-Mar) Several companies run boats from docks on the Dijver, Rozenhoedkaai and by the Blinde Ezelstraat bridge. Cruises depart approximately every 20 minutes in summer.
Horse-drawn carriage tours (€30 per carriage for a 30-min tour; ☼ about 9am-early evening, depending on demand) Touristy but historically informative tours setting off from the Markt.
Quasimundo bike tours (☎ 050 33 07 75; www.quasimundo.be; ☼ 10am-12.45pm Mar-Oct; €22 incl bike rental) Guided cycling exploring the Bruges backstreets.

ANTWERP
Bicycle tours Antwerp's tourist office (p197) has detailed maps with routes to discover the city by bike, and can also organise a guide.
Flandria (Map pp120-1, B3; ☎ 03 231 31 00; www.flandriaboat.com; booking office Steenplein) Runs 50-minute river cruises (1pm, 2pm, 3pm and 4pm daily Jul-Aug, Wed-Sun May, Jun & Sep, Sat & Sun Oct; adult/concession €7.50/6.50), and also offers 2½-hour port sightseeing tours (2pm daily May-Sep; adult/concession €12/10) and three-hour candlelight dinner cruises including wine (8pm 1st and 3rd Saturday of the month year-round; adult/concession €65/45).
River Tours (☎ 03 711 38 21; www .rivertours.be; ☼ May-Sep) Interesting

DIRECTORY

array of river cruises, including a coach trip to Brussels, guided Brussels walking tour then a river cruise back to Antwerp (€21). Call to book or book online.

GHENT

Several companies operate 40- to 50-minute **cruises** (adult/child under 12yr €5/2.50; 🕙 10am-6pm Mar-Oct); try **Gent Watertoerist** (Map p143, C2; ☎ 09 269 08 69; www.gent-watertoerist.be; departs Graslei) or **De Bootjes van Gent** (Map p143, B1; ☎ 09 223 88 53; www.debootjesvangent .be), departing from Kraanlei, just west of the Korenmarkt.

Mini-yacht rental (☎ 03 779 67 77; www .minervaboten.be; €47 for two hr; 🕙 by reservation). You don't need a licence or prior experience to pilot your own way around Ghent's waterways.

Yummy Walks (☎ 09 233 76 89; www .vizit.be; nibbling tour €10, dinner tour €55; 🕙 nibbling tour 3-5.30pm Sat, dinner tour 6-10pm Sat) Taste regional specialities on a nibbling tour with stops at traditional stores to try fine cheeses and meats, and Belgian chocolates and sweets, or enjoy a moveable feast on a dinner tour, stopping at four different restaurants for a course and drink at each. Both tours depart from the tourist office (opposite).

SMOKING

In 2007, restaurants in Belgium became smoke-free. But unlike a growing number of European countries, this law hasn't extended to cafés and pubs that are primarily drinking establishments (including those that serve food), at least for the time being.

TELEPHONE
MOBILE PHONES

Belgium uses the GSM 900/1800 cellular system, compatible with phones from the UK, Australia and most of Asia (and all tri-band phones), but not GSM 1900 phones from North America (GSM 1900/900 phones are OK), or the separate Japanese system.

PUBLIC PHONES

Public telephones accepting stored-value phonecards (available from post offices, telephone centres, newsstands and retail outlets) are the norm.

COUNTRY AND CITY CODES

Belgium's international country code is ☎ 32. Area codes for each city are incorporated into telephone numbers. You must dial the area code, even when dialling from within the relevant area. Telephone numbers given in this book include the necessary area codes.

USEFUL PHONE NUMBERS

English-speaking directory assistance operator (☎ 1405)
International access code (☎ 00)
International operator (☎ 1324)

TIPPING

Tipping is not obligatory, as service and VAT are included in hotel and restaurant prices. It's common to round up restaurant bills and taxi fares by a euro or two. In public toilets people are expected to tip the attendants (€0.30 to €0.50).

TOURIST INFORMATION
BRUSSELS
Brussels International Tourist Office (Map pp40-1, B6; ☎ 02 513 89 40; www.brusselsinternational.be; Hôtel de Ville, Grand Place; 🕙 9am-6pm) has stacks of Brussels-specific information and brochures such as *Your Capital City*. *Your European Village* (€4), a handy cartograph pop-up guide to the city.

BRUGES
Bruges' main tourist office, **In & Uit Brugge** (Map pp102-3, B6; www.brugge.be; 't Zand 34; 🕙 10am-6pm Fri-Wed, 10am-8pm Thu) is located inside the contemporary, redbrick Concertgebouw (Concert Hall). In the train station there is also a small **tourist office** (Map pp102-3, B8; 🕙 10am-5pm Mon-Fri, 10am-2pm Sat & Sun).

There are no phone lines for the public into either tourist office branch, but during business hours you can call the marketing back-office of **Toerisme Brugge** (☎ 050 44 46 46) for assistance before and during your visit.

ANTWERP
Tourism Antwerp (Map pp120-1, C3; ☎ 03 232 01 03; www.visitantwerp.be; Grote Markt 13; 🕙 9am-5.45pm Mon-Sat, 9am-4.45pm

Sun & holidays) also has a branch at Centraal Station which keeps the same hours.

GHENT
Ghent tourist office (Map p143, C2; ☎ 09 266 5660; www.visitgent.be; Botermarkt 17; 🕙 9.30am-6.30pm Apr-Oct, 9.30am-4.30pm Nov-Mar) is in the historic centre.

TRAVELLERS WITH DISABILITIES
Belgium's centuries-old buildings pose the biggest difficulty for travellers with mobility problems. Some public buildings, museums, hotels, restaurants, cafés and arts venues have lifts and/or ramps, but the majority don't. A 2000 law obliges architects to ensure buildings including hotels and shops are built in a 'disabled-friendly' way, but this will take time.

Outdoors, wheelchair users are up against uneven cobblestones, narrow pavements and steep kerbs. When travelling on the national railway, wheelchair users must give an hour's notice. The website for Belgian Railways (p188) has detailed information for mobility-impaired passengers. Alternatively, contact their customer service department for further information. Only a handful of Brussels' metro stations have lifts (elevators), but this number is gradually increasing. Likewise,

Brussels' new leather-seated trams (p76), which are currently being rolled out, are wheelchair accessible. Check with MIVB/STIB (p187) for updates.

Flanders' bus operator De Lijn (p187) aims to make all of its buses accessible to wheelchair users by 2010.

Attempts have been made to assist the visually impaired, such as Braille plaques at the entrance to some Brussels metro stations.

In this book, we've used the symbol ♿ to denote wheelchair-accessible sights, but check ahead regarding specific requirements. Many restaurants may only have partial access and restaurant bathrooms may not be large enough for wheelchairs or provide rails – ask when you book.

Taxi Hendriks (www.hendriks.be, in French & Dutch) have taxis in Brussels (☎ 02 752 98 00), Antwerp (☎ 03 286 44 40) and Ghent (☎ 09 216 80 20) that accommodate wheelchairs.

INFORMATION & ORGANISATIONS

Accessible Travel Info Point (☎ 070 23 30 50; www.accessinfo.be) Information for Flanders.

British Royal Association for Disability and Rehabilitation (RADAR; ☎ 020-7250 3222; www.radar.org.uk)

Irish Wheelchair Association (☎ 01 8186 400; www.iwa.ie) In Ireland.

Mobility International (☎ 541-343 1284; www.miusa.org) In the USA.

>INDEX

See also separate subindexes for See (p203), Shop (p205), Eat (p206), Drink (p207) and Play (p208).

000 map pages

INDEX

🔍 SEE

000 map pages

🏠 SHOP

🍴 EAT

000 map pages

000 map pages